FROM AMERICAN IDOL

TO

BRITISH ROCK ROYALTY

THE AMAZING STORY OF

ADAM LAMBERT

FROM AMERICAN IDOL

TO

BRITISH ROCK ROYALTY

THE AMAZING STORY OF

ADAM LAMBERT

BY

NEIL DANIELS

From American Idol To British Rock Royalty – The Amazing Story

Of Adam Lambert

First edition published, 2015

ISBN-13: 978-1507866009

ISBN-10: 1507866003

Copyright Neil Daniels © 2015

Visit Createspace at *www.createspace.com*

Visit Neil Daniels at *www.neildanielsbooks.com*

CONTENTS

PUBLISHED BOOKS BY NEIL DANIELS

PRAISE FOR THE AUTHOR'S PREVIOUS WORKS

ALSO AVAILABLE FROM NEIL DANIELS BOOKS

INTRODUCTION

Adam Lambert's story is truly inspirational.

As a talented albeit humble and shy kid with a natural flair for theatrics and a stunning voice, he was destined for stardom at an early age. Even before entering *American Idol* he had carved out a career in theatre from amateur and semi-professional musicals to fully-fledged big money productions such as *Wicked* and *The Ten Commandments*, Lambert's voice and persona amazed everyone in anything he did. And then of course *Idol* came along and he wowed the judges and audiences with his terrific performances, though he did not win the competition. Still, as is the case with talent shows the runners-up have become more successful than the actual winners.

Since his *Idol* days, Lambert has recorded two solo albums which have sold millions and at the time of writing a third album is on its way for a 2015 release. He is a rare pop artist in that his music appeals to young people because of its dance beats and funk vibe but with his love of classic rock and his awesome renditions of well-known rock numbers he has grabbed the attention of older music lovers.

Singing with KISS and Queen on *Idol* proved that he has the chops to sing rock music, so much so that he fronted Queen in 2012 and then on a major tour of the world in 2014 and 2015, which pretty much made him a household name the world over. It certainly broadened his appeal in the UK. Critics and fans raved about his performances.

Queen fans were initially dubious, though, about the band hiring a talent show runner-up to front their beloved Queen especially as the collaboration Queen and former Free and Bad Company singer Paul Rodgers didn't go down so well. It has to be said, Queen are not the only major rock band to hire tribute singers or talent show winners and the like; Judas Priest and Journey are just two examples. But Queen have picked the right man for the job this time around. Having seem them live I can attest to that. He's no Freddie Mercury, but he is not meant to be. Neither are they a tribute band. I was blown away by the band's performance and Lambert's showmanship at the Manchester date in the UK in January 2015. He has the voice, the image and the theatrics to perform Queen songs with aplomb. My only criticism is that he is not a seasoned enough performer to have authority over such large audiences, but of course that will come in time. Hopefully there will be more Q+AL tours and even an album at some point.

Lambert has also dedicated much of his free time to various charitable courses and helped raise the profile for gay performers. He has become something of a modern day role model.

From America Idol To British Rock Royalty charts Lambert's rise from his humble beginnings in San Diego to worldwide stardom. It is not just a biography; there is also a timeline of important dates in his career, a section on trivia, a list of some of his influences, some quotes from the man himself and a discography. It's a handy book for Glamberts and a nifty introduction to his life and music for newcomers.

Thank you to Chris Mee for the previously unpublished photos of Q+AL taken at the Glasgow 2015 date.

Enjoy.

Neil Daniels

February, 2015

www.neildanielsbooks.com

PART ONE

BEFORE THE MUSIC

Adam Lambert was born on January 29, 1982 in Indianapolis but raised in San Diego, California. His mother, Leila, was an interior designer while his father, Eber, of Norwegian descent, was a program manager for Novatel Wireless. Lambert had a pleasant and supportive upbringing with his younger sibling, Neil.

Lambert spoke a little bit about his origins to the *LA Times'* Fred Bronson: "I believe I was conceived on their honeymoon in Puerto Rico. I should have a little T-shirt that says, 'Conceived in Puerto Rico.' They had me about nine months after their wedding.

My parents moved me out of Indianapolis when I was about a year old. My mom and dad said: 'This isn't the right fit for us. We want to go somewhere else.' So a job opportunity opened up for [my dad] in San Diego and we moved."

Much of his childhood was spent in North County but when they initially moved to San Diego they based themselves in Rancho Bernardo but then when he was around five years old they moved to Rancho Peñasquitos before settling in Del Mar after his brother was born.

Lambert was raised Jewish, though he was never bar mitzvahed and detested Hebrew school which he left around aged 9 (some reports suggest 5), and sang songs in Hebrew such as 'Shir LaShalom' and 'The Prayer'. He later performed at the 2005 tribute concert to the assassinated Israeli Prime Minister Yitzhak Rabin and then at the San Diego Temple Of The Arts.

"We did celebrate Chanukah as opposed to Christmas," he said to Gail Zimmerman of the *Jewish Journal* in 2009. "So we stayed true to our roots that way. And we celebrated Passover occasionally. I mean I hate to say it, but we were kind of Jewish by form. Lightly Jewish. Diet Jews. More of a heritage thing."

From a young age Lambert was interested in the arts and performing so much so that he began performing at the Metropolitan Educational Theatre Network (MET2). He was merely nine years old.

Leila spoke to Angela Ebron *Womans Day* about what her son was like as a young boy: "He was very precocious. I took him to a lot of plays and concerts when he was small, and he always found a deeper meaning in them while I always took things literally. One time we went to see *Les Miserables* when Adam was 8. Afterward, he went into this elaborate discussion about how things were staged. He was so inquisitive, always asking questions. When he was about 5 years old he asked, 'If God is in the sky, how does he see through the roof?' I had to tell him, 'I'll get back to you on that.'"

He immersed himself in local productions such as *You're A Good Man, Charlie Brown* and *Fiddler On The Roof.*

Aged 10 or 12, his performance in *Fiddler On The Roof* showed that he really did have talent even at such a young age. His parents were in the audience and after Lambert belted out a song, they were like, "Where did that come from?". They were taken aback by his vocal talents. In *Fiddler On The Roof* he got to show off his vocals in the scene during the 'L'Chaim' number. The parents of his fellow cast members and director were held in awe of his voice. Even back then he was making a name for himself.

Theatre was a natural fit for Adam Lambert. His parents did not know what to do with him at first because he had so much energy and because he was so hyper. He wasn't into sports, swimming or club scouts. He was very creative at home and enjoyed playing dress-up and reciting scenes from films or TV shows so the theatre became his calling. As he entered his teenage year's people began to take notice of him and learn that he could sing. Singing came natural to him, he was very comfortable with it. He would sing along to recordings of some of his favourite musicals such as *Rent, Grease, Miss Saigon, Jesus Christ Superstar, Les Miserables* and his absolute favourite, *Phantom Of The Opera*, which he saw live for the first time at a theatre down in LA.

His first professional job was in a TV commercial. His mum had gotten him and his brother an agent in LA and head shots for the casting directors. They had to commute a lot to LA for auditions. His brother was also acting too and actually got more gigs than he did.

Lambert told *LA Times'* Fred Bronson: "It was a Century 21 commercial. I must have been 11. I ran around with a dog in the front yard and they did a crane shot. I was out of school for the day and I thought it was the coolest thing. That was the first professional thing."

Lambert loved movies too and the pop culture of the time.

He spoke to *Holy Moley's* Tim Chipping about his favourite childhood toy: "Skeletor's castle. It was He-Man and She-Ra, and the villain was Skeletor and he had this castle – it was like a set piece where you could play with the action figures on it.

You remember how there was a microphone at the back with an echo sound? And there was a cage where you could put slime on the guys that got caught in there. And there was a face in the wall – like a puppet – and you could make it talk. You know me, I was a pretty imaginative kid and I wanted to make-believe everything."

Lambert was always very close to his mother. There was one time for Mother's Day when he was 15, he gave her a card and on it was a flower on the cover and the petals had been taken off and stuck inside with a poem saying how much he loves and appreciates her. Needless to say she kept it.

He was 16 years old when he decided he wanted a tattoo. The tattoo on his wrist means the eye of Horus and it means protection. He actually wanted to have the Cantonese word for 'creative' but his mum told him that to be creative you don't have to be labeled as such. Rightly so. So instead she got a canvas and her neighbour to spell out the word in Cantonese and have it painted on for his seventeenth birthday. He kept it in his bedroom.

He was actually born a redhead, though he has always experimented with his hair dying it different colours and styling it in different ways.

"I really struggled with my self–image for a long time," he

said to Nancy Jo Sales of *Details* in 2009. "I thought I was ugly. So that's probably where all the makeup and the dyeing of the hair stemmed from."

Lambert was educated at Mesa Verde Middle School and Mount Carmel High School where his performing, acting and vocal coaching practices intensified. Competition was hard, often brutal. Talent teachers can be extremely tough on the kids offering fierce criticisms and applying too much pressure on the children, their students. His mum helped out with fundraising dinners, offered moral support and helped out behind the scenes, though she did not sneak into rehearsals like some of the other parents.

He took part in the Broadway Bound Youth Theatre and he performed with the school jazz band and local productions, both amateur and semi-professional. The jazz band was excellent experience for Lambert because he got to perform with a full band, which featured a revolving line-up of guest speakers. He was also learning how to work with a full orchestra as the productions he was involved with became more professional.

It was at The Starlight venue where he did his second professional gig after the TV commercial from a few years back. He was about 16 and it was for a theatre company in Balboa Park.

He was also cast in an ensemble for *Hello, Dolly!* and *Camelot* and the following summer he did shows at the Moonlight Amphitheatre in North County. Other shows included *The Music Man, Grease* and Captain Hook in *Peter Pan*.

As after after-school activity, Lambert was a member of Metropolitan Educational Theatre for eight years, which was run by a man named Alex Urban. Lambert also got to work with a voice teacher named Lynne Broyles. Aside from the aforementioned drama and theatre clubs and jazz band he was also in a high school project called Air Bands, which is a very popular competition in San Diego. It's like staged music videos with storylines that involve chorography, costumes and lip-synching. Lambert really enjoyed it and the tips he learned would prove useful for the future. He also learned how to use his ear and harmony; it was like singing with a choir.

Lambert didn't struggle through High School; theatre was his savior, as he told *Today Online*'s Farah Daley: "I didn't go through some of things I've heard some kids have gone through. I mean, it helped that I grew up in a more liberal area of San Diego but middle school years were a bit awkward. I was kind of a loner. My way of dealing with it was pulling a way, which is not the best way. As I got a little older in high school I realized communities are really important. If you find an activity that you really, really love then chances are you'll find somebody else who really loves it and you'll bond over that. And that was kind of my saving grace, being involved in choir, drama, photography and student council, things like that where there were like-minded people and we got along."

His main music love during this period was mostly pop, in particular modern divas like Missy Elliott, Britney and Christina as well as boy bands such as 'N Sync and Backstreet Boys.

Lambert was 17 when his mum went to a gay and lesbian centre in Hillcrest to talk to a counselor about so she could get some advice on how to approach him about it. They told her not to (some men never tell their parents regardless of how old they are) but as she knows her son better than anyone else in the world, she did speak to him and it turned out to be totally the right decision. Lambert came out when he was 18, though it did not become public knowledge until he became famous with *American Idol.*

Lambert graduated in 2000 before he attended California State University in Fullerton but left after just a few weeks to pursue a career in the entertainment biz. He wanted to go to NYU and Cincinnati; he applied for them but he wasn't accepted.

Homework was just a distraction. He wasn't interested in education, he had set his sights on the theatre. New York and Broadway, in particular. He wanted his name in lights.

Lambert spoke about this period to Lina Lecaro of *LA Slush*: "I dropped out of school right away because I wanted to continue theater, I wanted to keep working. I was in a show at the time, playing a supporting part, getting paid. It was *Grease* down in San Diego. I thought, I'm getting paid, doing this 'semi-professionally,' so why can't I keep pursuing this? So I moved up here to keep pursuing it, lived in a little apartment on Cahuenga in the Valley that was like a roach motel, it was so rundown. And then I got a job for a cruise ship, worked for about 10 months. Came back and lived in another apartment on near Lankershim, so I was in this little neighborhood for a little while."

College wasn't for him. It was a bold move, but one that would pull off.

IT'S HAPPENING

"The last 18 years of my life, I've been learning and I want to live and I want to go and be in the real world," he explained to Fred Bronson of the *LA Times*. "And I had sat through a couple classes and I thought, 'I'm not going to learn anything here. They're saying stuff that I already know.' I was being a little bit ridiculous, and I learned the hard way that it doesn't really work that way. I left school and my dad said, 'I'm not paying your bills. You've got to get a job.' So I got a job working at Macy's in Orange County at the Main Place mall right near Fullerton. I was doing retail and I stayed there for about six months and then I moved to North Hollywood. I had a couple friends that had moved up. I hung out with them and I was miserable. I couldn't find a job. I couldn't work. I was fat. I was a little lonely, and then I got my first job, which was on a cruise ship. I was 19."

Indeed, Lambert was just 19 years of age when he landed his first professional paid job at a cruise ship (Holland America) for ten months with Anita Mann Productions. Anita really liked his voice which is how he got the gig. It was a tough gig because he was young and his fellow cast members were dubious of him so he had a lot to prove. It was also difficult because everything went so fast – he had a lot to learn in a small amount of time. He was not yet fully confident in himself and he felt overwhelmed. After the first night, where he gave a stellar performance, the cast were a lot friendlier and chatty with him.

"That showed me the world," he said to Nancy Jo Sales of *Details* in 2009. "And I got to do a lot of shopping. It affects your perspective like crazy. Somewhere in the South Pacific I saw a really poor Third World island and I was like, ohhhh. I had never seen that. I was kind of, like, upper–middle–class and white–bread."

He was on the ship for ten months and he got to see Russia and Scandinavia, the Mediterranean, the Caribbean and the Pacific. The East Coast as well as Hawaii and then down into Australia and New Zealand.

However, it was around this time while in Europe on the cruise ship production that he learned his parents had split up. It is difficult for anyone, child or adult, to cope with their parents separation.

Aged 19, he decided to move to LA to pursue his dreams. He lived in a dingy apartment infested with bugs, there was a cracked window behind the dusty curtains. His parents were horrified. He then went on to perform in light opera in Orange County and by 21 he was signed with a manager and cast for six months in a European production of the famed musical, *Hair*.

He spent six months in Germany (mostly Berlin but also Hamburg and Munich) and craved to stay in Europe. In Germany, the producer decided that the dialogue had to be in German and as no one spoke German a coach was hired to teach them phonetically. Needless to say it was a disaster. If someone didn't know a German word they said it in English. Still, it was a learning curve for Lambert. He also spent time in Italy and Amsterdam during the production of *Hair*.

During this period, the shy kid from San Diego lost his virginity. It was a period of growth, both personally and professional, for him.

Professionally, it was really happening for Lambert. He did some more theater work and was auditioning for parts all the time which was very draining. He was involved in a Reprise Production over at UCLA. It was called *On The Twentieth Century* with David Lee, the director. By this point his Equity card had arrived which meant he was a professional actor. He was getting good wages and able to afford his way in life by paying bills and the rent.

In 2004 he was cast in a production of *Brigadoon* by the Theatre Under The Stars before moving onto the Pasadena Playhouse production of *111 In The Shade*. He was then cast in the role of Joshua alongside Hollywood star Val Kilmer in an ill-fated production of *The Ten Commandments: The Musical* at the famed Kodak theatre.

Lambert played Joshua and as with the cruise ship gig he had a lot to prove, as he explained to the *LA Times'* Fred Bronson: "Everything was copacetic by the end, but in the beginning, I was doing all this promotion for them to get interest built for the show and singing the song everywhere. I was on the Chabad Telethon and I was in love with being a rock star and I was going to rehearsal with nail polish on and eyeliner from the night before, and the director came up to me and said, 'Could you take all that off?' and I asked, 'Why?' He told me, 'The producers are a little uncomfortable with it. They don't really get it,' and I said, 'But we're not in costume yet. Why does it matter?' He said, 'They feel like you're supposed to be the leader of the Hebrew army by the end of this and they're really uncomfortable with the way it looks.' And I told him, 'This is theatre. This is a pop musical. What ... is your problem?'"

He got to make friends with Val Kilmer, though they soon lost touch. He hung out at Kilmer's house and it was Lambert's first taste of fame. People took photographs of themselves with Lambert and asked him for his autograph. It was a real eye opener for him and it was a glimpse of what life would be like in the spotlight.

It was during this period when he got out of his first serious relationship and sank into something of a depression. To combat his sadness he went out all the time and lived a fruitful hedonistic lifestyle going out to parties and enjoying LA's nightlife. It was wild. He loved the music and energy of the clubs.

Other musical performances in the mid to late 2000s included the *Upright Cabaret* and the *Zodiac Show* which was co-created by Carmit Bachar of the Pussycat Dolls. It was in the Zodiac Show at the Music Box in LA where he got to sing Sam Cooke's 'A Change Is Gonna Come' in full glam attire.

"That's the thing about me…I was a chorusboy for work and by late night, I was a club kid," he said to Lina Lecaro of *LA Slush*. "So I was like going out after the show and getting dressed up a lot. I was really into Miss Kitty's [Parlour] too because that's where I lived, right around the corner [near the Dragonfly]."

Right after the *Zodiac Show*, Lambert was continuing to gain the attention of LA casting agents and production managers so much so that the casting director for *Wicked* hired Lambert as the understudy for the role of Fiyero in the first national touring production of the revered musical in 2005. It was another major break for Lambert.

The Ten Commandments set him up for *Wicked* because the casting director was aware of the positive reviews he got. *Wicked* was a Broadway production of the highest sort even though it was on tour and it was a production that *The Ten Commandments* had tried – but failed – to be.

He would return to *Wicked* for the 2007 LA production and is said to have earned $1,800 a week as an understudy. His association with the musical ended in 2008.

Because he was in an ensemble he got to go out onstage every night even though it wasn't always as Fiyero, which he only went onstage as a couple of times. They rehearsed up in Toronto for a month or so before it opened and after two months or so in Toronto they performed in Chicago for a couple of months and then LA and San Francisco. After about six months he felt as though he had had enough with *Wicked*. He actually felt as though it was a step down from *The Ten Commandments* because he was not as well featured, however, he had achieved his goal of being in a Broadway Production. Lambert decided he wanted to be a rock star so he dropped out and pursed a career in music. He became interested in recording.

Indeed it wasn't just musicals and the theatre that Lambert was interested in.

Lambert's love of rock music came from his dad's 1970s record collection which featured the likes of Queen, Aerosmith, Led Zeppelin and David Bowie.

"My dad was a college DJ," he told the *LA Times'* Fred Bronson, "so he had a really huge record collection and he is very proud of it. There was always music playing in the house, all vinyl. He was a Deadhead, so there was some Grateful Dead, which I never really got into. There was a lot of classic rock. Bob Dylan.

Bob Marley was playing a lot. My dad has really good taste in music."

Lambert was also hooked on the music (and style and image) of pop icons Madonna and Michael Jackson. His favourite rock singers included Freddie Mercury, David Bowie and Robert Plant. He was a huge fan of the British glam rock scene of the 1970s especially the Ziggy Stardust era of Bowie's career. He would spend hours listening to Queen and mimic the vocals of Freddie Mercury, though he did not properly devour the band's music until his early twenties. The flamboyance of Mercury and Bowie also had a profound impact on Lambert.

Like many of his American peers, Lambert first discovered Queen after watching the 'Bohemian Rhapsody' scene in the 1992 Mike Myers and Dana Carvey comedy *Wayne's World*. He asked his dad about the song and his dad told him that they wrote 'We Will Rock You' and 'We Are The Champions'.

Queen's career in the US had taken a nose-dive after 'I Want To Break Free', a famous music video where members of the band dress as women mimicking the British TV soap *Coronation Street*. Middle America thought that Mercury might actually be gay. The band didn't want to work so hard to get their audiences back and so they concentrated on other parts of the world where they were filling stadiums and selling millions of albums. They hoped a hit record would resurrect their career in America. It didn't happen. However, *Wayne's World* and the publicity surrounding Mercury's death did boost their appeal in the US which is when Lambert and other music fans his age learned about them.

"When I was older I got more into the history of rock," he said to *Rolling Stone*'s Andy Greene in 2014. "I fell in love with the 1970s and I discovered more about Queen. The genius about the band is that they're so versatile. There are songs in their catalog that are like beautiful lullabies, and then on the same album they can flip to a hardcore, more aggressive sound."

Because of his dad's record collection he didn't listen to the radio that often but he did visit the Warehouse where he would buy 2-for-1 CDs such as Paula Abdul's *Shut Up and Dance* remixes tape. He dug out an Elvis karaoke tape and some of the first CDs he bought were Wilson Phillip and Mariah Carey's *Emotions*.

The parents, liberal folks, of a female friend of his at a theatre group would have parties where the soundtrack would be

'60s and '70s music from the likes of the Stones, Dylan, The Doors, Zeppelin, Hendrix and Joni Mitchell. He even formed a band with her dad called the Gutter Rats or Vicarious. They wrote some original songs together and recorded them on a six-track tape deck. It was like a garage band. Fun stuff.

Lambert also fronted the rock band The Citizen Vein with Steve Sidelnyk, Tommy Victor and Monte Pittman but it didn't work out and the band folded though they made some rough recordings. They performed just three gigs: the first at the Knitting Factory and then at the Cat Club on Sunset Boulevard and at some club in Hermosa Beach.

Guitarist Monte Pittman, a former member of Prong and live guitarist for Madonna and Adam Lambert, spoke to *Kings Of A&R* about The Citizen Vein: "I had an awesome band I played in when I lived in Texas called Myra Mains. I played in that band since I started learning how to play guitar. When I moved to LA, I wanted to start a band. Of course, touring with Madonna or Prong took up a lot of time. I used to play with Club Makeup which went on every month in LA. There were different themes each month and had some of the best singers I've ever heard. I asked one of them if he had any recommendations for a great singer and he suggested Adam. We later met while performing for a show called The Zodiac Show which started kind of when Makeup stopped."

He later learned about Mercury's' sexual orientation but believes sexuality or gender should not be an issue because it's the music that matters.

"It doesn't have to matter whether you're gay, straight, bi, black, white, whatever, man, woman. That's not the point," he said to the *Advocate*'s Daniel Reynolds in 2014. "That's not the thing that's bringing us together. The thing that's bringing us together is music. [We're] entering a period of time now where we're getting towards that post-gay sensibility, which is, so what? But it took a lot of fighting to get there."

Many of his musical heroes came out of the 1970s, mostly from the glam scene in England or in Detroit and New York.

"What's funny is that in the '70s a lot of the glam artists – like Bowie, T. Rex, Iggy Pop, Alice Cooper, KISS – they were gender bending with their image, but most of them were pretty hetero." *Out*'s Shana Naomi Krochmal in 2009. "Even though they looked really flamboyant. Bowie was the one guy that kind of made you wonder. But he was straight, right?"

His obvious love of classic rock and pop is what would help him carve out a career in the music industry, and ultimately what would make his name on his major breakthrough, which was just a round the corner.

Around this period he was desperate for money and the jobs were thin on the ground so he took part in a production of *Debbie Does Dallas* in Lake Tahoe at a topless revue at Harveys Casino. Again, it was with Anita Mann Productions. It wasn't a good job for him though as most of the audience just wanted to see topless women. This is when he decided to re-join *Wicked* after he heard they were hiring in LA. He had been out of the touring company for around a year.

Lambert also took gigs as a demo singer and session musician with his producer pal Monte Pittman.

He stayed for the entire LA run and loved every minute of it especially as he lived just down the street from the theatre. The money was good and he got to stay at home in his city. On the side, he hooked up with a producer who was forming his own company making film and TV jingles and advertising campaigns and started working on his own recordings. Lambert was hired as a songwriter. He went down to the studio a couple of days a week and laid down some recordings and over time he started to build a collection of original songs. He learned how to write lyrics and arrange music and create pop hooks and such. It was a very interesting and creative time. However, he became unsatisfied with *Wicked* as he felt they were not promoting him enough. He started to perform at clubs to get his name out there. He had two dancers and they wore crazy clothes and they did stuff with Upright Cabaret. He set his sights on becoming a solo act even though there were lots of productions that were interested in him as a musical actor. He didn't want to be an actor and he was becoming more disillusioned with musical theatre.

Adam Lambert turned 26 and pop stardom beckoned.

AMERICAN IDOL

Adam Lambert's major career breakthrough was just around the corner.

26 years-old, he auditioned for the eighth season of the popular TV talent show, *American Idol* in San Francisco.

Such was his situation that he decided to go for the *American Idol* audition after attending an arts festival (said to be the Burning Man Festival in the Nevada desert where he is reported to have tried acid for the first time) where he had an epiphany and concluded that if he wanted to achieve his dreams and ambitions he just had to go for it.

After he arrived back home, he made a plan to start various projects and when he heard there was an audition for *Idol* he decided to go for it because he could not sit around waiting for it (success) to happen.

Another reason why he decided to audition was during season seven he would watch the show with his buddies from *Wicked* and they would discuss why some contestants would do better than others. His buddies suggested he should audition. He thought, why not?!

He drove up to the audition in San Francisco with his two best friends, and after the audition he was so anxious that he only got an hour's sleep. He had reached a sort of epiphany in life – he was working, he had a resume filled with productions and musicals and could afford to pay the bills but he wanted to do something great and to make a name for himself on his own terms. *Idol* would be the platform for success, a way to launch himself. And if he wasn't going to be successful on *Idol* at least it could enhance his theatre career. In a sense it was a win-win situation.

In his audition he sang 'Rock With You' and 'Bohemian Rhapsody' which advanced him to the Hollywood stage where he sang 'What's Up', 'Believe' and in a group effort, 'Some Kind Of Wonderful'. Simon Cowell had some minor complaints about the theatricality of his vocals but Randy Jackson offered more acceptance. Nevertheless, he advanced to the next round of 36 finalists who performed '(I Can't Get No) Satisfaction', a favourite song of his mum's who had seen the Stones in concert. Lambert was subsequently voted into the Top 13 finalists. He was suddenly thrust into the limelight.

He spoke to *Out*'s Shana Naomi Krochmal in 2009 about the knowledge he had accumulated during his twenties whilst working in the industry which made him savvy towards the business suits: "I've been in the theatre industry for a long time. And I've lived in LA for eight years. And when you're in the city of entertainment, and you open your eyes and you meet people and you hear stories and you have friends that have been through this and that, going onto a show like *Idol*, you get it, going into it. I think what happens is that a lot of people that they get are from a small town in the Midwest, or they were a student and now they just kind of sing on the side. The whole amateur aspect of the show is really interesting, because it creates accessible personalities for the audience to attach themselves to."

Now it was down to the first week of live shows, where he had to truly show his talents as not only a singer but as a performer.

He worked with musical director Rickey Minor and vocal team, Dorian Holley and Michael Orland on arrangements. Generally, they would look at the original song and cut it down to one minute and 45 seconds and figure out the arrangements to make it flow and do things with his voice to make him stand out amongst the others in the competition.

His version of Michael Jackson's 'Black Or White' won

him praise from all four judges and for the country music themed week he sang a sitar-based rendition of 'Ring Of Fire'. He liked the idea of taking a country song and rearranging it to make it non-country. He heard a version of 'Ring Of Fire' by a woman named Dilana on the *Rock Star: Supernova* show. It had a Middle Eastern dub feel which he loved. He was also inspired by David Cook's re-worked version of 'Billie Jean' from the previous season. Lambert polarized people with his take on the Johnny Cash number, it really pushed the judges and audiences buttons. He set himself apart from his fellow contestants and it worked. It got everyone talking and it made him realise that he could play around with his song interpretations and image more than the initially thought.

Of course his family were there all the way.

"Unfortunately, both of my mom's parents have passed away," he said to *Jewish Journal*'s Gail Zimmerman. "My dad's parents are both alive, and they've been blown away by everything that's been going on. I saw my grandma at one of the California shows. I think she came to the second LA show, and she was so sweet. She really enjoyed that."

Cowell was not a fan of the version but it won praise from

Randy Jackson, DioGuardi and Paula Abdul. Lambert then performed an acoustic version of The Miracles; 'The Tracks Of My Tears' which won a standing ovation from Smokey Robinson who was the week's mentor. Lambert was now down to the Top 8 finalists. He sang the Michael Andrews and Gary Jules version of 'Mad World' which received a standing ovation from Cowell, something he had never done before on the show. It's a very haunting and beautiful song and something very different from what is usually performed on *Idol*.

Lambert then progressed to the next stage and sang 'If I Can't Have You' which again won great praise from the judges while his version of Led Zeppelin's 'Whole Lotta Love' heavily lauded by Cowell. Advancing to the next stage he sang 'Slow Ride' with Allison Iraheta which got him down to the Top 3. He next performed 'One' and then 'Cryin'' which got him into the final.

Lambert made a visit to his hometown and sang 'Black Or White' and 'Mad World' at his alma mater, Mount Carmel High School. Such was the respect and excitement in San Diego that the mayor Jerry Sanders declared May 8, 2009 'Adam Lambert Day'.

By the end of the season he had become far more comfortable on a soundstage in front of the cameras. He would watch himself on recorded episodes and learn what he did right and where he was going wrong. Sometimes he would be too bubbly and jittery because of nerves but as the season developed he became more at ease. He was learning a lot about himself. The director of the show Bruce Gowers was very helpful by giving him advice and ideas and telling him how to make the most of the format. Ken Warwick, the producer, was also extremely supportive.

In the finale of season eight of *America Idol* Lambert performed three solo songs, 'Mad World', the 1960s Civil Rights anthem 'A Change Is Gonna Come', which he had sang onstage earlier in his career though he changed a lyric for *Idol*, and 'No Boundaries' which would be the winner's mandatory single.

Not only did Lambert sing three solo songs to great reverence from the judges, including Simon Cowell, but he performed a medley with rock band KISS featuring 'Beth', 'Detroit Rock City' and 'Rock And Roll All Nite'. It was a brilliant performance that gave KISS frontmen Paul Stanley and Gene Simmons a run for their money.

"This can sound very pretentious if taken the wrong way but I almost feel like I've been preparing for this my whole life," he enthused to Fred Bronson of the *LA Times*. "I do feel this is what I'm supposed to be doing and I have a fatalistic view on life that things happen for a reason. I feel like everything that's led up to this point has prepared me for this. It's the whole *Slumdog Millionaire* thing, where it's like his whole life like leads up to that moment and the only way he gets through that moment is because of all of his experiences. I went to see *Slumdog* as this was all happening and I was just in tears because I was so touched by the concept of that movie. And I wouldn't have done what I did on the show had it not been for what I've gone through and my experiences in my life and what age I'm at. I wouldn't have been that confident. I would have been second guessing myself. I would have been really busy people-pleasing as opposed to just doing what I do. It was meant to be now."

He was then joined by Kris Allen and Brian May and Roger Taylor of Queen to perform 'We Are The Champions' during the finale.

"Oh my god, what an honour," he said to *Entertainment Weekly*'s Adam B. Vary in 2009. "Queen is like one of my all time favourite rock bands, and then to be up on stage with KISS with the pyro and the costumes – I mean, it was a dream come true. It was awesome."

Unfortunately Lambert did not win the competition, losing to Kris Allen and coming second in the overall votes.

"The first thing I did in the morning was crack a Red Bull," he said to *Rolling Stone*'s Vanessa Grigoriadis in 2009 about the morning after the finale. "For a little while, I felt I was at a rave. Then I went from 'Oh, my God, who has glow sticks?' to 'Stick a pacifier in me, I'm done.'"

Lambert's version of the winner's single was released alongside Allen's own take on the song. Lambert was ranked fifth in *The LA Times'* poll of the Top 120 *American Idol* contestants from seasons one to nine, above Allen.

It's doubtful that Lambert would have done so well in earlier season of *Idol* had he auditioned when he was younger because it took him time to shape and refine his talent and to build up confidence. Working in various theatre productions thicken his skin and made him stronger and less immune to criticism.

"I got to sing every week, work the system, it's a game,"

he said to Caroline Frost of *Huffington Post* in 2012. "As somebody who watched the show, I was always yelling at the screen, disagreeing with the judges, and their opinions are valid, but it's so subjective, and what you hear sonically is really different on TV."

Lambert liked Allen as a person and was pleased that he won it. There was no jealousy or animosity, at least not publically. Lambert is too grounded, affable and humble to bitch in public.

"We were roommates, so we were kind of thrown in together, and he's just like a really open-minded, good person," Lambert said to *Entertainment Weekly*'s Adam B. Vary in 2009. "He's got a great view of the world. We share a lot of philosophies on the world, even though we have different backgrounds. You know, I've learned a lot about his relationship with his wife. She's great. We've hung out. He's just a good guy, you know?"

He didn't feel any pressure, though. He took all comments and criticisms as a means to support and encourage him. He felt that anything aimed at him could be seen as a positive and that it would really help him in the long run. He felt that he could take risks and had it not been for that support he would not have done so well in the competition.

Lambert spoke to Arnold Wayne Jones of the *Dallas Voice* about the advice he received during *Idol*: "I had a lot of support from my circle of friends who were like, 'Just do what you've always done. It doesn't matter that you're on TV now; just do what you've always known.' The hardest thing about the show is all of a sudden, there's all this pressure and all these factors that you aren't used to as a performer, and you have to tune it out and just trust your own gut and try to maintain that sense of integrity. And it's not easy. Then, transitioning into the music industry is the same challenge. You're like, 'OK, well, I gotta play the game but I also want to do what I want to do, so how do I do that?"

During his run on *American Idol* he sang a variety of songs either solo or in a group efforts, those numbers included 'Rock With You' by Michael Jackson, Queen's 'Bohemian Rhapsody', 'What's Up' by 4 Non Blondes, 'Some Kind Of Wonderful' by Soul Brothers Six, Cher's 'Believe', Rolling Stones' ('I Can't Get No) Satisfaction', Michael Jackson's 'Black Or White', Anita Carter /Johnny Cash's 'Ring Of Fire', 'Tracks Of My Years' by The Miracles, 'Play That Funky Music' by Wild Cherry, 'Mad World' (originally by Tears For Fears), 'Born To Be Wild' by Steppenwolf, 'If I Can't Have You' by Yvonne Elliman, 'Feeling

Good' by Cy Grant, 'Whole Lotta Love' by Led Zeppelin and Foghat's 'Slow Ride', 'One' by U2 and Aerosmith's 'Cryin'', 'A Change Is Gonna Come' by Sam Cooke' and the original AI single 'No Boundaries' as well as Queen's 'We Are The Champions' with Queen and KISS's 'Beth', 'Detroit Rock City' and 'Rock And Roll All Nite' with KISS.

Because of his success the 2005 sessions that he recorded when he was a struggling singer and theatre performer were released on a compilation in 2009 on the album *Take One* by Rufftown Records. It reached Number 72 on the *Billboard* 200 and by January 2010 had sold 40,000 copies in the US.

In response to the release of the unofficial album, Lambert issued a statement through 19 Entertainment stating: "Back in 2005 when I was a struggling artist, I was hired as a studio singer to lend my vocals to tracks written by someone else. I was broke at the time and this was my chance to make a few bucks, so I jumped at the opportunity to record for my first time in a professional studio. The work I did back then in no way reflects the music I am currently in the studio working on."

The album features 'Climb', 'December', 'Fields', 'Did You Need It', 'More Than', 'Wonderful', 'Castle Man',

'Hourglass', 'Light Falls Away', 'First Light', 'Want' (December Remix), 'Spotlight' (Did You Need It Remix), 'On With The Show' (Fields Remix).

The reviews were somewhat dubious, understandably.

All Music's Stephen Thomas Erlewine said: "The songs aren't horrible but they're not memorable and neither are Lambert's performances, but that's unfair to him: these recordings were designed to sell middle-of-the-road pop with commercial aspirations and have absolutely no room for flair, since the whole point is to showcase the lyric and melody. Lambert acquits himself in that regard, sounding like nothing more than a demo singer because that was, after all, what he was."

Emusic's Amelia Raitt wrote: "*Take One* shows a more modest, less glittery side of the star, but even before there was a 'Glam' in 'Glambert', his vocals were spot-on. A sign of the great things to come. He might not ooze sexuality from every camera-ready pore on this recording, and it may not be the most artistically risky thing he's ever done, but for insatiable Glambert fans *Take One* is a must-have."

Lambert was a controversial contestant after photos of him kissing another man were printed during his *American Idol* run which did not please conservative voters but Lambert admitted the photos were of him and that he had nothing to hide about his sexuality.

He spoke about this with *Out*'s Shana Naomi Krochmal during a 2009 interview: "There was never any deliberate, like, 'I'm going to hint now' because I was never in the closet. The funny thing about dealing with all that was…When those pictures came out online, I got freaked out. I was like, 'Great, that's gonna fuck things up.' 'Cause I just figured, you know, this is a national television program and people are conservative in our country, aside from LA and New York and a couple of other places."

He officially confirmed that he was gay in an interview with *Rolling Stone* in 2009.

For *Rolling Stone* to interview Lambert, essentially a runner-up in a TV talent contest, was a major coup. He was blown away by the offer; it shook his world. Lambert was very honest and open during the interview, even though his mum had always told him to be discreet with whatever he does and say. But it is in Lambert's nature to be open and forthright. It makes him a genuine character.

Leila spoke to *North County Times'* Pam Kragen about it: "I was so happy that our families got along so well. The night after the finale was my birthday and the Allens came to my birthday party, not just Kris and his wife, but his brother and his parents. We're also planning to meet up at one of the tour stops this summer and go see the concert together. When the *Rolling Stone* article came out (featuring Lambert lying on his back with a large python coiled near his crotch), she called me and said, 'I love your son but I don't like the *Rolling Stone* cover, only because I don't like snakes.'"

He chose to tell-all in the interview rather than doing a series of low grade celebrity gossip magazines, he wanted to choose one of America's most prominent cultural voices, *Rolling Stone*.

"I find it very important to be in control of this situation," he said to *Rolling Stone*'s Vanessa Grigoriadis in said 2009 piece. "I feel like everyone has an opinion of me, and I want a chance to say, 'Well, do you want to hear how I really feel about all this?'"

As soon as he "came out" the media appeared to solely focus on his sexuality. A lot of good came out of it; when he was a kid there was no one he looked up to who had admitted their sexuality so for Lambert to do it meant that he could be a role model to young boys and girls who were struggling with their sexual identity. Lambert, nor any other pop star or artists in the limelight, is taught how to be a gay celebrity. One thing he did learn during this period was how to become more confident in the spotlight.

Simon Cowell spoke to *TV Guide* about Lambert's openness with his sexuality: "I think people only get bothered really when they know somebody's hiding something. (laughs) We've had that in the past! We've obviously never had an issue with it, and nor should anybody else. It's a huge step forward for the show. It's just, do you like him as a person, as a singer, full stop."

After the climax of the season Lambert performed 'Mad World' on *The Early Show* on CBS and the next morning he visited the studios of *Live With Regis And Kelly* where he sang 'Mad World'. He also performed a version of Muse's 'Starlight' on *Good Morning America*'s televised concert series in central park and was featured in ABC News' 20/20 and also performed on the American Idols LIVE! Tour in the summer of 2009.

A lot of sexual energy goes into his performance and during the *Idols* tour he was the subject of much adulation from female members of the audience as he explained to Nancy Jo Sales of *Details* in 2009: "I think it's weird that I'm having this effect on women. It's flattering. I've never had underwear thrown at me before. Clearly there's something significant about it, because there aren't a lot of openly gay men in the entertainment industry."

His solo spot included the Led Zeppelin song 'Whole Lotta Love', Muse's 'Starlight', 'Tears For Fears' 'Mad World', Foghat's 'Slow Ride' and a Bowie medley of 'Life On Mars?', 'Fame' and 'Let's Dance'.

During the tour he had already begun work on his first album, as he told *People*: "We did a lot of work on it right before the tour started. I wrote a lot with various producers and writers and recorded a handful of songs. We've been doing a lot of work on it during the tour as well ... We're still gathering material and we're scheduling more recording sessions for when it's over, so we're about halfway done."

He added: "There are songs on there that are anthems; there are song that make you want to dance; there are songs that make you feel sexy; there are songs that touch you, hopefully, with more emotional, insightful, deeper lyrics. There are songs that are more in the line with a rock sound. There are some that are really pop-oriented."

Leila, who had moved to LA to be near her son to give him support, spoke to *North County Times'* Pam Kragen about the reception he was getting on the tour: "Just before Adam was to appear onstage, the crowd went wild. The energy was so powerful. I was asked last night by one of the fans 'What was your favorite part?' and I would definitely say that as I stood there it appeared that everyone was on their feet. Watching Adam perform, I took a moment to do a 360-degree turn to take in the crowd and realized at that moment that Adam's dream had come true. He was singing 'Starlight' and I just started to cry. That was my favorite moment."

Lambert picked up mostly positive reviews from critics who had witnessed his performance.

The New York Times' Jon Caramanica wrote of the tour's stop at the Prudential Center in Newark: "Mr. Lambert, perhaps the most currently visible openly gay American musician, received a thunderous reception from the audience, far louder than that for anyone else. His mother, seated in the audience, barely had a moment to herself between camera-wielding fans. He had the sharpest merchandise, including a David Bowie-esque black T-shirt with neon accents."

Meanwhile the *Washington Post*'s Ruth McCann said of the Verizon Center gig: "After eight of *Idol*'s top 10 finalists had done their thing on Verizon Center's stage, Lambert appeared (cue shrieks) to open his mesmerizing set with Led Zeppelin's 'Whole Lotta Love', an ace in the hole, given that the crowd was liberally peppered with Adam Lambert T-shirts and signs that declared: 'Adam is my winner,' 'I {heart} Adam Lambert,' etc. So a song in which Lambert promises 'I'm gonna give you my love' was unsurprisingly successful."

The *Seattle Times*' Misha Berson wrote of the Tacoma Dome performance: "It's not overstating the case to suggest that Lambert really does have the makings of a revivalist, glam-metal rock avatar. The whisper-to-a-scream voice, the pouty sexiness, the elaborate makeup and Lizard King costuming, the androgynous sex appeal – it's all there, just like on the tube, but with wildly pulsating video and more smoke."

And continued: "By the end of his set, though, Lambert's shtick felt a bit too predictable in its conscious excessiveness. And though no entertainer in their right mind would want to follow his act, the casually attired (plaid shirt, jeans) Allen did so with amazing grace."

A fully-fledged celebrity he was now armed with a manager, PR and a bodyguard. He was living in a rented three bedroomed house in Hollywood Heights and drove a Jaguar coupe. Such was his growing reputation and fanbase that an army of fans dubbed the 'Glamberts' started writing fan fiction about him on the internet, which is not uncommon in the digital age. He's never let fame go to his head and inflate his ego; he knows he's not invincible.

He spoke to *LA Slush*'s Lina Lecaro about his legion of fans: "They're supporting my craft and my opportunities, so of course I support that. And again, it's case by case. I can't make a generalization about my fans or going out because it's different every time and everyone's different. I try really hard to take everything case by case, you know? And it's hard because in our celebrity culture in the way of the media, celebrities are kind of… labels are really easily slapped on people based on one-time things, and even if you have one negative experience with paparazzi or a fan or someone in a bar, suddenly you're 'that guy.'"

He Googles himself sometimes, depending on the circumstances but he isn't obsessed with getting his name further up the Google rankings. Sometimes he is just keen to know what people are saying about him. It's not vanity. He isn't vain. Twitter had changed him because he receives direct comments from his fans so he learns what he has done wrong, and he learns how to improve himself. He has direct contact with his growing army of fans and admirers.

Leila spoke to Angela Ebron *Womans Day* about what how her son handled fame during and after *American Idol*: "Although he can't always go places and he has to try to be more inconspicuous, he really appreciates the love and support of his fans. They have touched his life. Once when we were at a restaurant, a woman from another table came up and asked if he'd sing 'Happy Birthday' to her daughter. I said, 'No, we're eating,' but Adam said, 'It's OK, Mom,' and told the woman that he'd stop by after we'd finished. He went over in a little bit and sang to her daughter. It was a wakeup call for me."

His mum helps him out behind the scenes with the administrative stuff such as fan mail.

"The one I read was a little creepy," he admitted during an interview with *The Guardian*'s Michael Haan in 2012. "They always show me having relations with someone I have never – and would never – have relations with. I find it funny the fans get so wrapped up in those myths, but if they want to, they can go on fantasising about it."

Leia also helps out her son with general chores. There was one night Lambert needed a shirt for an appearance and he called his mum to ask her if she could iron it for him because he was busy in the recording studio. Leila continues to do general mum stuff.

Leila spoke to *North County Times*' Pam Kragen about it: "We're very close, but we won't live together. He doesn't need his mommy living with him, I'm quite sure. But there are a lot of things I could help him with because he's not going to be around a lot. The hardest part for me is moving. I love my house and it's hard to give it up, but I'm totally amazed that he wants me there. He wants me to be a part of it, and to meet the people he's meeting. There aren't a lot of kids out there who would want that. I'm so blessed. He's got a really big heart."

His brother, on the other hand, was living in New York as a journalist while his dad stayed in San Diego.

"You know, it's funny [but] my mom doesn't give me a lot of advice these days," he admitted to *Jewish Journal*'s Gail Zimmerman. "I think it's kind of in the vein of an unspoken kind of advice. It's more of a support thing. My dad's really Mr. Advice."

Lambert bagged two awards that summer: the Young Hollywood Award for 'Artist Of The Year' and the Teen Choice Award for 'Male Reality/Variety Star'. He'd also picked up one million Twitter followers.

"It's weird to know that I can just pick up my cell phone and on a whim, write something and a million people are going to read it," he said to *Hitfix*'s Melinda Newman in 2011. "It's kind of dangerous."

Lambert learned how to play the "fame game". He knew that the gossip rags would be all over him, and indeed they were. He handles it well, though; the fame.

He spoke to *Holy Moly*'s Tim Chipping: "I remember early on there was some article that was like: 'Adam Lambert's a total diva and he was bossing all of his people around'. It was completely fabricated and I was like, 'what? Where did this come from?' Gossip is silly. It comes with the territory. One person can say something to one magazine so that they can sell some copies. But there's no fact checking, there's no way to insure that truth is printed. It's all a game."

At six feet one inches tall and in good shape with stylish looks, he was appealing to both men and women and loved the adulation. As far as he is concerned it does matter whether men or women are screaming at him so long as they're having a good time.

"He's so confident and self-assured," *Idol* creator Simon Fuller said to *Rolling Stone*'s Vanessa Grigoriadis in 2009. "He's like Marc Bolan meets Bowie, with a touch of Freddie Mercury and the sexiness of Prince."

Closing the year he appeared on *Larry King Live* and announced that he was working on his debut album.

Asked if Lambert could be a star, Simon Cowell told *TV Guide*: "One hundred percent. He's somebody who should be selling records all over the world. He's that good. He could sing the phone book, and a lot of producers will want to work with him."

FOR YOUR ENTERTAINMENT

There's one revelation that came true for Lambert.

"You know, at the risk of sounding a little bit cliché, that anything's possible," he admitted to *Jewish Journal*'s Gail Zimmerman. "I really think that, to a point, if you dream something and really visualize it, I think that it can come true. I really do believe that now."

Lambert's debut album *For Your Entertainment* was released on November 23, 2009. It peaked at Number 3 on the *Billboard* 200 and sold 198,000 copies in the US in its first week of release. It was released in the UK on November 29 to positive reviews but it was only available on imports, however, it still managed to climb to Number 80. It charted well in Europe but faired even better in Asia, especially in Japan; a stronghold for many American and British artists.

Critics gave the album mostly positive reviews. Here are some snippets:

Leah Greenblatt of *Entertainment Weekly* wrote: "His voice, though supremely capable, doesn't really have a distinct character; it's like listening to the world's sauciest wedding singer.

But if *For Your Entertainment* material sometimes wears him rather than vice versa, he's still the belle of what turns out to be one heck of a glitter-pop ball."

Ann Powers of the *LA Times* penned: "It's tough to balance it with theatricality, especially in pop, where big statements usually tend toward the earnest and the sorrowful. When Lambert does work to be heartfelt, he tends to lay back. Two outstanding tracks on *For Your Entertainment* – 'Broken Open', which Lambert co-wrote, and Linda Perry's 'A Loaded Smile' – are calmly rendered ballads that blend the ethereal lushness of Eurodisco with the upwardly mobile elegance of the New Romantics."

The *New York Times*' Jon Caramanica said: "But Mr. Allen beat Mr. Lambert for a simple reason: he was a more palatable singer of songs that were popular. Which means that of the two, Mr. Lambert, the star, has more to prove on his debut album, *For Your Entertainment*. And the labour put in to that end is almost audible: this is an overwrought, clunky, only sparingly entertaining record, constantly in argument with itself."

Stephen Thomas Erlewine of *All Music* said of the release:

"Lambert sounds larger than life on these, just like he wants to be, and if there's no sense of danger here – whenever he dons his leather and his girlfriends put on their stripper heels, it's playacting drama club kids getting a kick out of their adopted roles – at least there's a lot of pure pop pleasure, more than any immediate post-Idol album has ever delivered."

Naturally cynics would assume that Lambert had little input on his debut album but they would be incorrect as he point out to *The Guardian*'s Michael Haan in 2012: "people perceive it to be about a svengali taking someone and plugging them into all this stuff and here's an album. Don't get me wrong. There was a lot of help involved, and there were a lot of songwriters involved, but I was making decisions: I like that song or I don't like that song. I wasn't being told what to do every step. I wasn't being controlled in that manner on the show, either."

The opus features collaborations with Rob Cavallo, Dr. Luke and Max Martin with songs written by Matt Bellamy, Ryan Tedder, Rivers Cuomo, The Darkness' Justin Hawkins (who also wrote 'Suburban Decay' which was not recorded in the end), Pink, Linda Perry and Lady Gaga.

Lambert has stated that he co-penned six of the album's 14

songs: 'Strut', 'Pick U Up', 'Voodoo', 'Down The Rabbit Hole', 'Aftermath' and 'Broken Open'.

The title-track produced by Claude Kelly and Dr. Luke preceded the album's release but had little impact on the charts yet it was the second single 'Whataya Want From Me' that made the Top 10 and had the most impact in the US and worldwide. It was also nominated for a Grammy for 'Best Male Pop Vocal Performance' at the 53rd Awards Ceremony. 'Time For Miracles' was also released as a single and was used as the end theme for the Hollywood blockbuster movie *2012*.

In total the album had three worldwide singles with 'For Your Entertainment', 'Whataya Want From Me' and 'If I Had You'. 'Sleepwalker' was released in some foreign territories' while 'Fever', 'Sure Fire Winners' and 'Aftermath' were released as radio singles in some countries. The market tends to dictate which songs should be released in certain countries.

The album features 'Music Again', 'For Your Entertainment', 'Whataya Want From Me', 'Strut', 'Soaked', 'Sure Fire Winners', 'A Loaded Smile', 'If I Had You', 'Pick U Up', 'Fever', 'Sleepwalker', 'Aftermath', 'Broken Open' and the bonus track 'Time For Miracles'. A later version was released with 'Master Plan', 'Down The Rabbit Hole' and 'Voodoo' with the extra UK track 'Can't Let You Go'.

As is seemingly the case with many successful modern albums, a tour edition was released in 2010 with extra tracks and live performances and music videos.

The guitar solo during 'Sleepwalker' was played by Orianthi who has since hooked up with Richie Sambora, both personally and professionally.

Lambert was averse to the idea of bringing politics into his music, as he explained to *Out*'s Shana Naomi Krochmal in 2009: "I do have a point of view. I may have something to say now and again. I just want people to enjoy the song and have a good time. That's what music is about for me. It's not so political for me. I may be the subject of something that's so political, being that we're in a weird time right now. And if I can indirectly open people's minds up and get them to kind of change their views a little bit, then I'm really thrilled with that. But that's not my mission. That's not why I'm doing this."

By April 2012, Lambert's debut album had sold close to two million copies. It was certified Gold by June 2010.

Lambert continued to stay in the limelight most notably after a somewhat controversial performance of 'For Your Entrainment' at the American Music Awards Of 2009 when he kissed a male bassist and grabbed the crotch of another musician.

He does not regret his performance.

"I knew that label would be attached to me from there on out, and I think people would jump to conclusions with that label," he said on *The Oprah Winfrey Show* in January 2010. "I've seen a lot of press where they say, 'openly gay singer Adam Lambert.' It's like the gay part comes before the singer part, and I'm like, 'That doesn't define who I am.'"

It wasn't planned, Lambert was on autopilot and before he knew it they were kissing. Some of the chorography in the routine was planned but not all of it. He was acting on impulse.

He spoke to Caroline Frost of *Huffington Post* in 2012 about the performance: "I don't know what came over me. I was in the audience and I saw Rihanna and Gaga's performances, and I thought 'I've got to bump it up a notch', because I was so inspired by their performances. The whole night blew me away."

He added: "It did me some harm and some good. It freaked some people out, but the conversation it started was fruitful."

The Parents Television Council urged viewers to complain to the FCC and ABC, the broadcaster, received 1,500 telephoned complaints and as such Lambert's planned performance on *Good Morning America* on November 25, three days later, was axed.

"I kind of asked for it in a way," he said to Matthew Breen of the *Advocate* in 2011. "Not everything is so premeditated as people think it is. There are things that just happen, there are things you just do. It was an impulse."

CBS, however, invited him to perform on *The Early Show* in the same day instead.

He spoke about the American Music Awards incident on *The Early Show*: "Just to play devil's advocate with you. Lady Gaga smashing whiskey bottles, Janet Jackson grabbed a male dancer's crotch. Eminem talked about how Slim Shady has 17 rapes under his belt. There's a lot of very adult material on the A.M.A.'s this year, and I know I wasn't the only one. I'm not using it as an excuse, and I didn't take any offense with those performers' choices."

He added: "If it had been a female pop performer doing

the moves that were on the stage. I don't think there would be nearly as much of an outrage."

One thing is for sure, Lambert always approaches situations – whatever they may be – with a level head.

"You have to make a choice: do I want to be this for the cause, or do I want to be able to run my business a certain way? It's difficult. It's really difficult," he said to the *Advocate*'s Daniel Reynolds in 2014. "But everybody's different and for me, personally, my journey has been, the minute I was able to discuss my personal life after *Idol*, I immediately discussed it, because I wanted to be out and open. That's the kind of person I am, and that's the statement I wanted to make. But it hasn't been without its challenges."

Lambert returned to the American Music Awards two years later as a presenter. Such was the fuss over his initial performance that it was included in *Billboard*'s list of 'Top Ten American Music Awards Moments' in November 2012 when the AMA's celebrated forty years.

He's never been a performer that goes for shock value, as he explained to *Dallas Voice*'s Arnold Wayne Jones: "No; I don't think, 'OK, I want to piss people off now' or 'I want to shock people.' I kind of, especially after the [AMAs], go with what I want to do musically. That's been more in the forefront for me in my decision-making. I think just kind of being, and being unapologetic for being, is a risk in and of itself in today's music industry."

Before, around and after the release of his album Lambert was heavily featured in the press. He appeared on the covers of various magazines such as *Entertainment Weekly* in May 2009, *Rolling Stone* in June 2009, which became the magazine's best-selling issue of the year, and *Details* in November 2009 which featured Lambert with a nude woman. He also appeared on the cover of *Out* magazine in 2009 in their 'Out 100' special issue. He was listed in Barbara Walters' '10 Most Fascinating People Of 2009' and interviewed on the show on December 10. He was even included in *People Magazine*'s 'Most Beautiful People 2010' and then in May 2010 Japan *Rolling Stone* featured him on the cover after his single 'For Your Entertainment' became a hit over there.

He was featured in *TIME* magazine's 'People Who Mattered' featured, as journalist James Poniewozik penned: "After *Idol*, he infuriated some viewers with a raunchy, grinding show at the American Music Awards on ABC. Rather than apologize, he charged a double standard for gay men while keeping a smile on his face: when Joy Behar told him, on *The View*, that he was 'not exactly a nice Jewish boy,' he quipped, 'I'm a little different. My dreidel spins the other way.' Lambert ended 2009 out, proud – and loud."

Not only was Lambert seemingly all over the magazines but he appeared regularly on TV included spots on *Late Show With David Letterman*, *The Tonight Show With Conan O'Brien*, *The Jay Leno Show*, *Chelsea Lately* and the season finale of *So You Think You Can Dance*. He'd also cropped up on *The Ellen DeGeneres Show*, *The View* and *The Oprah Winfrey Show*.

It seemed that Lambert was now a bona fide star and a household name in the States.

"The biggest change between before *Idol* and now would probably just have to be the level of notoriety. I mean, it changes everything," he told Oprah Winfrey on her show in January 2010. "I try to go throughout my daily life just as if nothing has changed, but you don't have much anonymity anymore, which feels really good. People come up, and say hi and they enjoy your work."

In December 2009 he hosted and sang at the radio-sponsored Jingle Bells in New York, Miami and Tampa.

Moving into 2010 and AOL Music played a five song mini concert on AOL Sessions while Lambert performance a small acoustic set for iHeartRadio and then played his first official headlining gig, which sold out, at California's Fantasy Springs Resort Casino. VH-1 resurrected the *Unplugged* series which Lambert helped to launch in March.

Lambert popped up on *American Idol* in April as he became the first contestant to mentor the performers during an Elvis themed week. He was honest with his criticism, calling finalist Andrew Garcia's version of 'Hound Dog' "boring".

He next appeared on MuchMusic Video Awards in Canada where he received the UR Fav International Video Award for 'Whataya Want From Me'. And then in June he launched his first tour called Glam Nation which also ventured to Europe and Asia.

Lambert officially announced the tour via his website on April 28, 2010. He said: "I hope the audience will be able to escape for a few hours and fall into a world full of glam, drama and excitement. I'm confident we've put together a show far beyond the price of the ticket. I'm looking forward to connecting with fans all across the world with this show."

The initial batch of USA tour dates ran as follows: June 4: Wilkes-Barre, Pa. (The FM Kirby Center For The Performing Arts); June 5: Sayreville, N.J. (Starland Ballroom); June 8: Toledo, Ohio (Omni); June 10: Council Bluffs, Ia. (Harrah's Ballroom); June 11: Manhomen, Minn. (Mystic Lake Casino Hotel); June 14: Columbus, Ohio (LC Pavillion); June 15: Milwaukee, Wis. (Riverside Theater); June 17: Hammond, Ind. (The Venue at Horseshoe Casino); June 18: Royal Oak, Mich. (Royal Oak Theater); June 19: West Toronto, Ontario (Molson Amphitheatre); June 22: New York, N.Y. (Nokia Theatre); June 24: Mashantucket, Conn. (MGM Grand Theater at Foxwoods); June 26: Atlantic City, N.J. (Borgata Spa & Resort – Event Center); July 15: Kansas City, Mo. (Midland Theatre); July 27: Costa Mesa, Calif. (OC Fair – Pacific Amphitheatre); July 28: Costa Mesa, Calif. (OC Fair – Pacific Amphitheatre); Aug. 13: Bethlehem, Pa. (Musikfest) and Sept. 18: St. Petersburg, Fla. (Tropicana Field).

The opening night at the Kirby Sports Centre in Pennsylvania sold out. It was a terrific achievement for the former *Idol* contestant. He was truly making a name for himself now, on his own terms.

The US leg was supported by Allison Iraheta (of *American Idol*) and Orianthi. Other opening acts included Seth Haapu (New Zealand), The Monday Box (Finland), Viktorious (Sweden), Random Hero (Germany), Mytoybox (England), Carrie Mac (Scotland) and The Canyons (Los Angeles).

The setlist ran as follows: a video introduction of 'For Your Entertainment' followed by 'Voodoo', 'Down The Rabbit Hole', 'Ring Of Fire', 'Fever', 'Sleepwalker', 'Soaked', 'Whataya Want From Me', 'Aftermath', 'Sure Fire Winners', 'Strut', 'Music Again', 'Broken Open' and 'If I Had You' with an encore of 'Mad World', 'Whole Lotta Love', '20th Century Boy', 'Enter Sandman', 'Purple Haze' and 'A Change Is Gonna Come'.

His band consisted of guitarist Monte Pittman, bassist Tommy Joe Ratliff, keyboardist Camila Grey, drummer Longineu W, Parsons III (from June 4 to September 15) and Isaac Carpenter (from September 17 to December 6) with backing dancers Taylor Green, Sasha Mallory, Terrance Spencer and Brooke Wendle.

Jim Cantiello of *MTV.com* said of his two night stint in NYC: "In fact, the audience was so enamoured with the magnetic performer on Tuesday night that one could hear a pin drop during an especially quiet moment as Lambert sang the theatrical

'Soaked' – save for one drunken patron screaming out the name of singer Klaus Nomi."

And continued: "Wednesday night's audience was especially raucous. The energy in the venue extended from the back row all the way to the front where a group of good-looking young men planted themselves, glued to Adam's every move."

USA Today's Brian Mansfield said of Lambert's visit to Nashville's Ryman Auditorium: "One of the best things about the live Adam Lambert experience is the way he has completely reinterpreted many of his songs for the tour. Anybody who comes in expecting the arrangements from *For Your Entertainment* is in for a big surprise. The songs the band performed acoustically, for instance, were great showcases for that voice, giving it plenty of room to play."

Miami.com's Howard Cohen reviewed the Hard Rock Live performance in Hollywood which was supported by fellow season eight *Idol* finalist Allison Iraheta as his opening act: "He performed for barely 70 minutes and, unlike the energetic Iraheta, wasn't on stage the entire time. A few too many songs were abbreviated and, unlike some dates where he sang covers of 'Mad World' and 'Whole Lotta Love' during the encore, Hard Rock fans only got one song at the end, a passable take on T. Rex's 1973 oldie, '20th Century Boy'."

And continued: "Lambert, by comparison, offered stilted, scripted platitudes, such as this disingenuous bon mot: 'he key to true love and making it work is loving yourself.'

Daytime television viewers get enough of that talk. When Lambert chose to sing he was amazing. Next time, more of that and more show, please."

Outside of his native USA, his planned Malaysia gig in October was hit with protests from an Islamist political party.

As reference in *The Guardian*, PAS youth leader Nasrudin Hasan said: "Adam Lambert's shows ... are outrageous, with lewd dancing and a gay performance that includes kissing male dancers, this is not good for people in our country."

Touring Asia was certainly a culture shock for Lambert especially when it came to trying the foods, which is totally different from the burger joints and fast food diners of the US. But the one thing he did learn is that music brings people together regardless of language or nationality barriers. People attend his shows just to have a good time; that's what live music does – it cheers people up.

Touring is a grueling experience for any artist but Lambert got himself in shape and has always looked after his voice. He tends to drink tea before a show to warm his vocals and does a short exercise routine to get the blood following. He'll do some warm-ups, nothing too strenuous as concerts can be rigorous for performers. He'll chill out in his dressing room to get mentally prepared for the evening's performance.

After Lambert's performance at the American Music Awards 2009 and some of the controversy on said tour, he felt there was possibly a bit of fear around his shows especially in America. Gay people, particularly in certain parts of his native country, are still trying to get accepted and acknowledged. It's almost as if they are a different species. There's been much progress over the years but there is still some way to go.

"I just feel like I spent the last couple of years negotiating and navigating through this – 'Hello, I'm a celebrity and I'm gay!'", he explained to Maura Johnston, *Village Voice*, 2012. "And I've heard, just talking to people, they're like, 'You know, Adam, with you it always feels like it's about your sexuality.' And there's only so much control I have over that. The media will treat me how they want to. I'm a pretty open book. I'm answering all the questions. And the sensational gay responses are the headlines of the articles, even though I talk about this, that, and the other thing."

The tour last for 113 shows, many of which sold out. He finished the road jaunt with two shows in Los Angeles.

The Indianapolis gig at Clowes Hall on August 31 was filmed for his first DVD release, *Glam Nation Live* and a 13 track CD. The DVD peaked at Number 1 on the SoundScan Music Video chart and hit Number 12 on the *Billboard* 2011 end of year music video sales chart.

Tanner Stransky of *Entertainment Weekly* wrote: "If there's any newish pop act worthy of a live release, it's *American Idol* runner-up Lambert, whose vocal acrobatics make this a terrific complement to his 2009 solo debut. Because he incubated before us in a perform-or-die setting, Lambert's ability to work a crowd is audible. Everything from his hit 'Whataya Want From Me' to his take on 'Ring Of Fire' sizzles more than the too-too-perfect studio versions. Bonus: *Glam Nation Live* includes an expertly produced DVD of the concert."

One contributor to *BlogCritics* wrote: "Lambert wraps up his *Glam Nation Live* performance with his most pop rock song, 'If

I Had You'. He gets the crowd up and hopping with this danceable hit. The images go from black-and-white to colour and add vibrancy to the song, and Lambert gets a little sexual with his dancers. The *Glam Nation Live* performance was fun and energetic. Lambert eats up the stage with his booming personality. In just over an hour you get a cool Adam Lambert experience, plus a few touring videos to wrap up your tour experience. This DVD comes with a CD, so you have all the audio from the concert."

The tracklisting features some covers and originals: 'Voodoo', 'Down The Rabbit Hole', 'Ring Of Fire', 'Fever', 'Tribal Segment', 'Sleepwalker', 'Whataya Want From Me', 'Soaked', 'Aftermath', 'Jamming With Lazers', 'Sure Fire Winners', 'Strut', 'Music Again', 'Meet My Band', 'If I Had You' and '20th Century Boy'.

Such was Lambert's rising star that another unofficial product was released. *Beg For Mercy* contains his pre *Idol* material and was issued in November 2011. It contains 'Beg For Mercy', 'Rough Trade', 'The Circle', 'Turning On', 'Just The Way It Is', 'Sacrifice', 'Pop Goes The Camera', 'MP3's Killed The Record Companies', 'Crawl Through The Fire' and 'Run Away'.

Lambert then released the EP *Acoustic Live!* on December 6. It sold 10,000 copies during its first week of release and hit Number 126 on the *Billboard* 2000. By December it had sold 17,000 in the US. Not bad at all for a mini-album. It features 'Whataya Want From Me', 'Music Again', 'Aftermath', 'Soaked' and 'Mad World'.

Jim Farber of the *New York Daily News* wrote: "Lambert's 'acoustic' CD makes good on the title claim as far as the instrumentation lies. But it's clear he had no intention of dialing down his vocals – a good thing. Bombast remains a virtue in Lambert's case. He's downright operatic in 'Soaked' and as wild as Freddie Mercury on 'Music Again.' All the stripped background does is give Lambert more room to trill and soar. No wonder his acoustic disc feels electrifying."

Such was Lambert's growing stature that he signed a worldwide deal with Kobalt Music Group, a global independent music publishing company, in January 2011.

In August 2011 he was the subject of a special episode of VH-1's *Behind The Music* documentary series which was followed by appearances on *E! True Hollywood Story* and CNN Talk Asia.

He then appeared as a mentor on The Hub TV Network's *Majors & Minors* series where who coached the child constantans.

He joined the remaining members of Queen, Brian May and Roger Taylor, in November 2011 for a performance of 'The Show Must Go On', 'We Will Rock You' and 'We Are The Champions' at the 2011 MTV Europe Music Awards in Belfast. Queen were handed the 'Global Icon Award'. Roger Taylor admitted in December that Queen were in talks with Lambert over a possible collaboration.

"There was stuff I really wanted to do on my own first," he admitted to *Rolling Stone*'s Andy Greene in 2014. "But there was definitely interest from me and the band. When we finally got together at the MTV Video Music Awards about a year or two after *Idol* it felt like the right time to start talking, since I'd established my solo career."

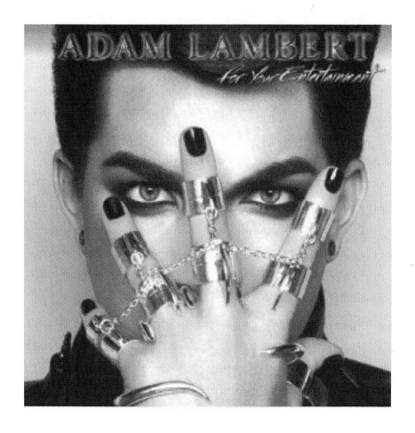

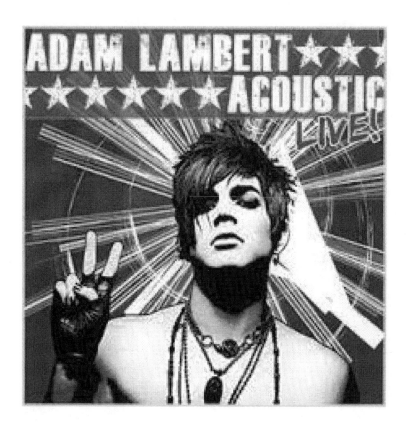

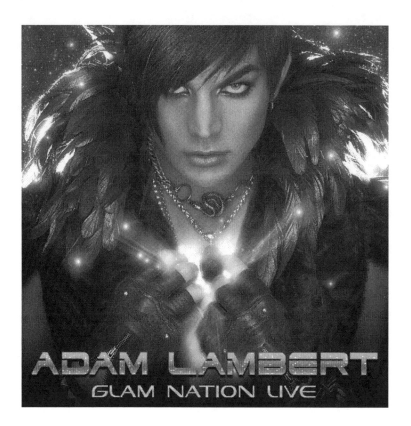

TRESPASSING

It was time for the so-called "difficult second album", but Lambert had no difficulties at all. For Lambert, each album is a progression and extension of the last one.

He spoke to *Hitfix* 's Melinda Newman in 2011 about his musical journey: "I think the most important thing for me to keep in mind as a songwriter and as a vocalist now is that my fans want to hear my voice, first and foremost. And I think kind of our general rule in songwriting is that it has to come from the heart; it has to be real."

Lambert announced the release of his eagerly awaited second album, *Trespassing*, in August 2011 after he switched from 19 Entertainment to Direct Management Group.

It was all happening so quickly.

Lambert was gearing up for the release of his second full-length studio album. In January he performed 'Better Than I Know Myself' on *The Tonight Show With Jay Leno* and *The Ellen DeGeneres Show*.

On January 29 he celebrated his 30th birthday by performing a low key five-song acoustic set at the Q-Showcase in

Zell Am See in Austria. He debuted the title track of his second album, *Trespassing*. He also performed acoustic sets in Germany and Sweden.

Not only was he going to release a new album, but after much press hype it was announced in February 2012 that Lambert would unite with Queen to headline the UK's Sonisphere Festival in July, however, it the entire festival was axed. Roger Taylor quickly announced that the band would perform with Lambert in Moscow with the addition of two shows in London and one in Kiev at Independence Square which would also feature Elton John as headliner in aid of the Elena Pinchuk ANTIAIDS Foundation. A fifth gig was added in Wroclaw while a third London show was added after the first two sold out.

"I still can't believe we're doing this," Lambert said to *Digital Spy*'s Robert Copsey. "It'll sink in eventually! All we've done is send a couple of emails back and forth, but we'll get down to serious rehearsals soon. They're such sweet guys – almost paternal – and they're doing this for the right reasons. They love what they do and they want to keep giving to the fans."

Lambert continued to promote his second album after its May release ahead of the Queen gigs and while Queen fans eagerly awaited the dates, Lambert was busy with his own band after he unveiled a new line-up with a lead guitarist, drummer, bassist, keyboard player and two female backing singers dressed in choir robes. He performed various promo gigs at night clubs and festivals throughout North America, Europe and Japan during the summer of 2012. Other gigs were played in China, Australia and South Africa throughout mid-2012.

The album's initial release date was March 20, 2012 but delayed until May 15 so Lambert could add some more tracks.

With that, he had time to go back to the album and change stuff with the producers, write new parts and sing new lines, adding elements and generally fine tune the recordings so that it was 100% to his approval. He played the album for friends, associates and colleagues to get their opinion which he trusted and respected.

When he sat down to write the songs he realised he was into more funky, disco type music than he had initially realised. He had time to experiment and work on different sounds and so the tracks just flowed. He created other tracks that were more expected of him in terms of the sound but he wasn't really drawn to that particular sound, so once he got the funk-disco vibe going it all felt more natural. Michael Jackson's *Off The Wall* and early Prince was a huge influence during the making of the opus. Lambert was proving himself as musician. He wanted people to get a real taste for who he is as a person and an artist. He wasn't just a one-shot pop star. He has a vision and there is substance to his music.

Trespassing was all about Lambert asserting himself as a musician and a person. He was still living in the shadow of *Idol* even though he had done much to prove himself. It is difficult for any aspiring pop star who has entered a talent contest such as *Idol* to gain creditability and reverence but Lambert had done it more than anyone else. Being signed to a major label, having his own team of people, and having a major second record proved that he was now mainstream.

Lambert served as executive producer on the opus, which is a major leap from a former *American Idol* contestant and after just one album, too.

Speaking to the *Village Voice*'s Maura Johnston in 2012, Lambert explained: "A little bit into the process I said, 'Look, I really want to executive produce this. I'm going to be able to make sure that it has a cohesive feeling.' When I went into my various writing sessions – some of which I sought out, some of [which] the label arranged for me – I brought that in and I would sit there and talk with the producer and say this is the music that is inspiring me, this is the sound I want to give it, and I think I helped steer the ship."

Working at Conway Recording Studios in Hollywood, Lambert had a daily routine.

"These are my days," he said to Matthew Breen of the *Advocate* in 2011. "I woke up, I got on my treadmill at my house this morning and ran for 20 minutes and got ready. I love this juice place. This is called the singer's remedy, and it's lemon and cayenne. It clears your throat and gets your cords ready. And it's something I actually do. And I need gas to drive. It's a normal day."

The title-track was written with Pharrell Williams, which Lambert felt would be the perfect title for the album because it's about him breaking down barriers and marching forward.

"That's kind of true of this whole lifestyle for me of being in the entertainment industry," he explained to Farah Daley of

TodayOnline, "and taking risks like going on *Idol* and different projects that I've taken over the last couple of years have all been challenges so *Trespassing* is kind of this call to arms to just go for it. It was autobiographical but I was also trying to find some kind of common ground with all of my fans because I think that even though we're all very different and we all come from different parts of the world, we all go through the same stuff."

Lambert learned a lot from Williams – the writer behind the mega-hit 'Happy' – an artist who doesn't over-think but goes with his instincts and follows the natural flow of things. The two artists have different ways of writing but they gelled and got along like life-long friends. They respect each other talents.

"We had a big conversation about the music industry and the business and being an artist," Lambert explained to *Dallas Voice*'s Arnold Wayne Jones, "and then on top of it, being somebody that's different, being a gay man and being in an industry where it's not very common, not very present. Kind of feeling like I'm gonna own this, march forward and ignore any kind of sign or person telling me no. I'm gonna do what I wanna do and not feel sorry for myself."

Lambert has been on an interesting and exciting journey since *American Idol*. Certainly, being a celebrity, people trespass into his life all the time.

With his second album, he wanted to make a collection of songs aimed at the LA clubs that he used to frequent. He wanted to make music for that crowd. In his younger days before *Idol* and before the fame he loved being in a club and dancing and so with *Trespassing* he wanted to capture that vibe and energy. There are influences from the 1970s straight through to the '90s with bits of funk and disco thrown in there for good measure. The production is heavy with electronic beats. There are songs for men and women, straight and gay and alternative. It's an album with no social barrier. His aim was to make people happy, to get them up and dancing and to celebrate his passion for music.

With *Trespassing* Lambert was showing the world how proud he is of his sexuality and his identity. There's a huge double standard in the industry – it seems okay for a straight artist to make double-entendres and sexual innuendo but when a gay artist does it, the media cause a stir. Lambert was aiming the songs at open-minded people, people who can relate.

"I'm so proud of who I am and I'm 100 percent positive about it and I celebrate it – but I also think it's a bit dated to harp on it and to lean on it and to constantly be defined by your sexuality," he said to Arnold Wayne Jones of the *Dallas Voice*. "I think that gay men and women who live their lives as gay men and women understand that and understand that it's just another part of who they are. Unfortunately, with some mainstream publications, it's such a novelty for them to be able to talk about it. It's such a hot-button issue that it becomes the focus of a lot of discussion."

Whereas *For Your Entertainment* was more of a guessing game with *Trespassing* Lambert had since took full control. He had everything planned and had copious amounts of ideas, all mapped out.

"I think if you have an artist that doesn't take the initiative or want to do it then you have to work with that," he told Dean Piper, the gossip columnist. "I needed some of that guidance and help on the last album. I wasn't in control of everything like I am now. There were certain things I wouldn't have done. I mean, I had ideas but on the first record there was only so much I could actually put out there."

Trespassing was a year in the making and would take

months of hard work promoting it around the globe but he had made an album that he remains immensely pleased with. An album that would appeal to lots of music fans. He wants his message to be heard. He draws inspiration from modern music and created a radio friendly album, not to cash-in but to please his fans and to make new fans.

Lambert talking to *LA Slush*'s Lina Lecaro: "I want to make music and perform it for my peers and for the community. And luckily we have this fanbase, The Glamberts, that are so die hard. The other thing I love is it's dance music and it's fierce and flamboyant, but it's also borrowing from the classics so I think a lot of people will get something from it. The front half of the album is the dance funky stuff, but the back half slows down a bit, borrows a bit from industrial, new wave kind of sonic stuff."

The lead single 'Better Than I Know Myself' was a collaboration with Dr. Luke and Claude Kelly which was issued digitally on December 20, 2011. The album cover was designed by artist Lee Cherry.

To promote the opus Lambert appeared on both *The*

Tonight Show With Jay Leno and *The Ellen DeGeneres Show*. He also appeared on radio and TV in Europe including a guest appearance on the UK's *The Graham Norton Show*.

Despite the publicity and praise around the second release, he was still very proud of his debut album.

"I think the first album is amazing," he enthused to *Hitfix*'s Melinda Newman in 2011. "I'm really proud of it. That was my first time out. We did it really fast. It had a ton of momentum behind it and I got to explore my glam rock, you know, my glam rock self, my T-Rex/Bowie/Gary Glitter/Boy George self and this album is going to be an evolution."

It took to get the album right. The difficult second album is a common theme with artists, some can never eclipse the first album (only if it is a good, successful release) while others take much longer to progress until they hit their stride. Lambert had released a strong, successful and critically acclaimed debut so he had much to prove with his sophomore release. His plan was to write and record as much as possible and whittle down the recordings to the best tracks, enough for a full album of strong material.

Lambert is someone who doubts himself but with

Trespassing he felt he had created a damn good album. He knew what he was doing and he knew what he wanted to say. He was more knowledge about the industry than he did when he made the first album and he is more grounded. He also knows his fans better. Since the first album he had toured and built up a fanbase and he did not want to let them down. He was more confident as a singer and songwriter and it shows in the material. He had more time to figure out his sound and to develop the music.

He spoke to Matthew Breen of the *Advocate* in 2011 about the album: "No matter what the genre is, it's all very personal, even on upbeat, fun tracks. The last album was a little bit more of a fantasy escape…even my image for that last album felt very theatrical and kind of over-the-top and intentionally tacky. I get a kick out of making artistic statements that are kind of ridiculous."

Trespassing could be the soundtrack to Adam Lambert's life. It has his thoughts and feelings in the lyrics and his love of various genre of music are laid out across every track from start to finish. It is everything he wanted it to be and more. It's kind of a throwback dance album but with a modern twist. It's fresh yet retrospective.

He spoke to *LA Slush*'s Lina Lecaro about *Trespassing*: "The beauty of this album is that, at the end of the day anyone can relate to it. It's not specific, it's about the human experience. What it could accomplish in the larger picture is to say 'hey you know what I'm different, I'm gay, and we go through the same shit. You feel the same way about relationships as I do, you want to go out and get drunk and get crazy too. You had your heart broken, too. It's kind of post-gay. It's a post-gay record.'"

Trespassing peaked at Number 1 in the *Billboard* 200 and sold close to 80,000 copies while it topped the US iTunes album chart. In the UK it peaked at Number 3.

The album was at first made available online for free. Given the rise of illegal downloading and streaming music it was a risky deal which could have affected sales, but his team made the right decision as the album sold well.

Hitting Number 1 in his native country was a great achievement for an openly gay singer; the first openly gay singer to achieve a Number 1 hit album, which was an angle that the media focused on.

Lambert expressed to *Digital Spy*'s Robert Copsey about his achievement: "That's been a really major milestone for me – I didn't even realise it hadn't been met. I feel honoured to be that person. The sexuality thing is interesting for me – I came out of the closet at 18 and dealt with all my identity issues then. Suddenly, ten years later, I had to do all the defining and qualifying all over again – where in my personal life it was just part of my normal conversation."

Lambert has never felt any desire – or pressure – to be political in his lyrics but what he has aimed to do is raise social awareness and to help young people who are struggling with their sexual identity. He doesn't teach people how to be gay, but rather how to open up and feel free. He's made mistakes too, and perhaps at times he struggles with being a role model, but his intentions have always been honourable. He's a down to earth guy and if he can help people along the way he will. Of course as he has gotten older his perspective on life as changed and he wants to share his experiences with those who are struggled in life. Everyone has a divine right to marry whomever they want to, and someday Lambert would like to get married and raise a family.

The media are obsessed with his sexuality and have sensationalised it when the general public stopped caring and just appreciated his music.

He made a valid point during an interview with *The Guardian*'s Michael Haan in 2012. "Sexuality is a hot topic, so there's a natural interest. But the interest comes predominantly from the media. I've done lots of interviews and often that is the pinnacle of the article, or the headline, or the main angle."

Not only was Lambert pleased with sales of the record but also the positive reaction it received from the press. The album was given the thumbs up.

Shirley Halperin of *The Hollywood Reporter* enthused: "Glamberts should be pleased – there's plenty of uptempo glittery pop along with more revealing ballads all of which showcase Lambert's ridiculous range."

Rob Sheffield of *Rolling Stone* said: "It was his warmth, his humour, his burlesque bravado. His 2010 debut, *For Your Entertainment*, was a typical *Idol* quickie – decent, but it needed more personality. *Trespassing* delivers, with a mix of tinsel disco-club sleaze and leather-boy love ballads."

Glenn Gamboa of *Newsday* wrote: "Unlike his debut, tellingly titled *For Your Entertainment*, Lambert's new album, *Trespassing*, (RCA) sounds strictly for himself – a well-crafted collision of electronic dance pop and upper-register, booming

vocals mostly about pushing the envelope and enjoying life."

Slant Magazine's Jonathan Keefe said: "While that may

bode well for Lambert's commercial prospects, neither of those

tracks allows his distinctive talents to shine. When Lambert's

collaborators both employ strong hooks and capitalize on the

singer's irrepressible presence, however, *Trespassing* marks a

strutting step forward for Lambert."

The album consists of 'Trespassing', 'Cuckoo', 'Shady',

'Never Close Our Eyes', 'Kickin' In', 'Naked Love', 'Pop That

Lock', 'Better Than I Know Myself', 'Broken English',

'Underneath', 'Chokehold' and 'Outlaws Of Love' with bonus

tracks on the deluxe edition featuring 'Runnin'', 'Take Back' and

'Nirvana' and 'By The Rules' and 'Map' on the UK edition.

For Your Entertainment relied on a glam rock sound but

with his second opus he turned to pop, funk and dance oriented

beats. Lyrically, Lambert chose to explore more personal feelings

as many of the songs reflect his then relationship with Sauli

Koskinen, the Finnish reporter (and 2007 winner of Finland's *Big

Brother)* with whom he began a serious relationship with after

meeting in a bar. It was his second serious relationship and it kept him grounded and changed his perception of things especially fame and celebrity status.

"I think when I was single I was looking for validation in other ways and not in the most emotionally healthy ways," he admitted to Dean Piper, the celebrity gossip writer. "I think when you're single and looking for some sort of connection it was easy for me to feel lonely and insecure. All people seem to do things to fuck themselves up a little bit – and me included. There were elements of self sabotage on my part. It definitely goes there."

The first half of the album is fun and upbeat with dance beats which is cool to listen to when driving or running on a treadmill while the second half enters an altogether different sort of territory.

Lambert said to Emily Extor of *Pop Dust* in 2012: "I'm always listening to what's current – Top 40 for the most part. One of the things we explored on this album was a funkier sensibility. I was really diving into Prince and Rufus and Michael Jackson, some of his earlier stuff, and then [into] kind of a '90s world [with] George Michael and later Michael Jackson. There's a little Nine Inch Nails energy in there, too."

'Naked Love' and 'Shady' are especially personal, the latter is about the night they first met. There are light and dark tones to the album, reflecting love, marriage and anxiety. 'Outlaws Of Love' is about legalizing gay marriage.

"If I'm listening to an Adele song, which is written by a woman for a man," he said to *Details* in 2014, "I can relate to it also, and so can a straight woman, and a straight men, so why can't a gay artist have that same kind of universal appeal?"

The album's second single 'Never Close Our Eyes' was written by Bruno Mars and produced by Dr. Luke and released digitally on April 17. To promote its release he appeared on *Jimmy Kimmel Live!* and *Good Morning America.*

"Nowadays in pop, there's not a lot of men that are singing big and loud and high – it's not as common as it once was," Lambert told *NPR*'s Guy Raz in 2012. "So I got this track from Bruno and I thought, that's a great melody, great lyric – I know how I want to sing it. I want to sing it big."

For the third consecutive year Lambert made a return visit to *American Idol* on the results show before the final week to perform 'Never Close Our Eyes'. He had become a favorite not only of the show's creator Simon Fuller but also of the judges and more importantly, the viewers.

Lambert appeared at the Rays Of Sunshine Children's Charity at London's Royal Albert Hall before kicking into the impending Queen dates.

"It's a very intimidating venue as it's so huge with a lot of history," Lambert expressed to *Digital Spy*'s Robert Copsey about performing at the prestigious venue. "It was great to play my music to a crowd who don't necessarily know my music that well. There were some serious fans there, but the majority of the audience was hearing me for the first time, which is always a great experience."

The Queen + Adam Lambert collaboration brought him to the forefront of the rock music press. Mercury would probably approve of Lambert, at least as far as Lambert and many Queen fans think, though there will also be sceptics.

"I'm an artist, you know," he expressed to the *Village Voice*'s Maura Johnston in 2012. "My goal is to do the songs justice and not stray too far. I don't want to sacrilege; I want to keep the intent. I mean, I have Brian and Roger on stage, in rehearsal, telling me green light or red light. So I'm going to look to them in hopes of being kinda like, 'Hey, is this cool?' And I'm their guest."

The mini-tour commenced in Kiev with their first full gig as Q+AL on June 30 the night before the Euro 2012 Football Championship. The Moscow gig took place on July 3 at Olympic Stadium while the Poland event on July 7 took place at Municpal Stadium. The collaboration took some heavy criticism in the UK where Lambert was not so well known and where Queen are hailed as one of the greatest rock bands in the world. Why would they hire a former *American Idol* contestant to front the band?

Nevertheless three sold out Hammersmith Apollo gigs took place on July 11, 12, and 14.

The London shows featured classic Queen songs in a truly awesome setlist: 'Flash' (intro), 'Seven Seas Of Rhye', 'Keep Yourself Alive', 'We Will Rock You' (fast version), 'Fat Bottomed Girls', 'Don't Stop Me Now', 'Under Pressure', 'I Want It All', 'Who Wants To Live Forever', 'A Kind Of Magic', 'These Are The Days Of Our Lives', 'Somebody To Love', 'Love Of My Life', ''39', 'Dragon Attack', 'I Want To Break Free', 'Another One Bites The Dust', 'Radio Ga Ga', 'Crazy Little Thing Called Love', 'The Show Must Go On' and 'Bohemian Rhapsody' with an encore of 'Tie Your Mother Down', 'We Will Rock You' and 'We Are The Champions' with the usual recorded climax to a Queen show, 'God Save The Queen'.

The reviews were much better than expected, as evidenced here:

The Guardian's Caroline Sullivan reviewed one of the London gigs: "It's no insult to Lambert, a theatrical pop star in his own right, to say he lacks Mercury's magisterial authority. The late singer still inhabits every one of Queen's songs, and the best Lambert could do was sing them with verve. While vocally equal to the crescendos and curlicues, he was unable to compete with Mercury's memory – something vividly proved during 'Love Of My Life', when 1980s footage of Mercury unexpectedly flashed on screen. The crowd's gasp spoke volumes."

The Daily Telegraph's Neil McCormick wrote: "Hand-picked by guitarist Brian May, Lambert can certainly handle the vocal range of Queen's songs although he sings in a softer, more soulful, modern pop style, without Mercury's rock grit or operatic bombast."

He continued: "But it is to his credit that he is a talent in his own right and not just an impersonator. If his performance seems to improve as the show goes on, it's hard to be sure if that is a sign of Lambert finding his mojo, or the audience tuning in to his particular brand of flamboyant showmanship."

Indulge-Sound's Emma Webb enthused: "It was clear to see that having Adam fronting Queen for these shows was a spectacularly brilliant choice of vocalist; with his own little twist on songs including a sped up version of 'We Will Rock You' and providing us with a British accent before belting out 'Fat Bottomed Girls', he did not want to mimic Freddie (as let's face it, no one can) but he merely wanted to do him, the fans and the band proud and he went down a glamorous treat."

Lambert was praised by his friends and collaborators too.

"Pharrell [Williams] and I started talking and he said I was our generations Freddie Mercury," Lambert told celebrity gossip writer Dean Piper. "That was ridiculous. You're never going to replace Freddie in any way. But I'm thrilled to have the chance to do stuff with them. I can't wait to work with them again."

Adam Lambert is far more suited to the look and sound of Queen than former Free and Bad Company singer Paul Rodgers. The Queen + Paul Rodgers collaboration took place between 2004 and 2009 and spawned two major world tours and a lukewarmly received album called *The Cosmos Rocks* as well as a live album called *Return Of The Champions* and a CD and DVD named *Live In Ukraine*.

"Paul has one of the greatest rock voices but it's more blues- and soul-orientated I would have thought," Taylor told the *Toronto Sun*. "I would say, with all due respect to Paul, that Adam is more suited to a lot of our material and whereas we had great tours with Paul, I think Adam is more naturally at home with us."

"Yeah, I think the styles match more closely in a sense," May echoed to the *Toronto Sun*. "But we had a great time with Paul, no doubt about it, and it kind of stretched it to a new place and, I think, a thoroughly good experience. But Adam is really... Like us, he has many, many colours, so we can explore some of those strange excursions that Queen likes to."

It is clear that not only do May and Taylor appreciate and admire Lambert as a singer and artist but they also like him as a person.

Reflecting on the collaboration, Brian May spoke to *Ultimate Classic Rock*'s Annie Zaleski in 2013: "I would love it to happen. Since we did the iHeartRadio Festival, there's been a lot of talk and yes, we're looking at it to see what we could do. I don't think we want to press the button to do nine months on the road like we used to do, because we did that for so many years, but I think a few choice dates could be great. We're looking at it, and I certainly hope that we'd be able to come up with a scheme that works. Yeah, we love Adam, we really do. Like you say, he's the whole deal – he's an extraordinary singer with an extraordinary instrument. He's an entertainer, he's original and he's a nice guy. That's very important these days. If you're going to work with someone, you've got to enjoy them as a person and we certainly do."

After the Queen dates he continued his solo career which continued to thrive.

The title-track of his second album was released as the third single as part of an eight track EP of remixes and radio edits called *Trespassing Remixes*, which came digitally out in October. Hard copies were sold exclusively via his website. It hit Number 1 on the *Billboard* Hot Dance Singles Sales chart which was his tenth overall Number 1 *Billboard* entry. The EP features 'Trespassing' (Pharrell Radio Mix, Benny Benassi Remix, Zak Waters Radio Mix, Vanity Machine Remix) as well as two remixes of 'Never Close Our Eyes' (R3hab Remix, Mr. Mig & Mike Rizzo

Radio Mix) and one mix each of 'Better Than I Know Myself' (Robert Marvin & Shearer Remix) and 'Pop That Lock' (Johnny Labs Extended Mix).

To promote 'Never Close Our Eyes' and his second album he appeared on a Halloween special of *Pretty Little Liars* on October 23. iTunes named the album in its list of 'Best Pop Albums Of 2012'.

His schedule continued to be full with performances in South Africa in November and headlining arena dates in Cape Town and Johannesburg before travelling to Hong Kong to perform at the Mnet Asian Music Awards which was viewed by 2.3 billion people.

Lambert was invited to host the 2012 VH-1 Divas concert in December which included tributes to soul divas Donna Summer and Whitney Houston. He performed with Keri Hilson and Kelly Rowland and opening the show with renditions of David Bowie's 'Let's Dance' and Madonna's 'Ray Of Light'. The concert was in aid of VH-1's Save The Music Foundation which supports music education in public schools.

Lambert wrapped up 2012 with heaps of praise and adulation from the music and entertainment industry pundits. He was in many end of year lists and pills such as *Rolling Stone*, *Billboard*, *People*, VH-1 and Ryan Secrest.com. The Queen + Adam Lambert shows was named 'Best Live Act' of the year by *Gigwise* and one of *Classic Rock* magazine's top events of 2012.

Singing live in a studio or an arena is often hard work – the acoustics can be poor, so you have to be disciplined and patient. It's something Lambert was very professional about. Lambert studies his performances, looks at what he does wrong and improves himself. He is always striving to be a better artist.

Some of the year's standout solo performances included Summer Sonic Festival in Tokyo and Osaka and an acoustic performance at Sydney's Top 40 Lounge where he sang Bob Marley's 'Is This Love'. In appeared at the finale of *The Voice Of China* in September, becoming the first Westerner to perform on the show which was watched by 520 million people. He performed 'Whataya Want From Me' with a contestant and 'Trespassing' on his own. He later returned to mainland China for a headlining gig in March 2013. As a former *American Idol* runner up he was doing remarkably well overseas. He closed 2012 with a special New Year's Eve concert in Bali where he was on vacation.

"I think, for the majority of my twenties, I was always so concerned with what I didn't have, or what I still wanted," Lambert told *NPR*'s Guy Raz in 2012. "It was always about a chase and going after something. This year I've focused more on being thankful for what I already have – being content with what I've already accomplished, or who is already in my life, not what I've yet to find or get."

2013 kicked off with news that Lambert was going to leave 19 Recordings but remain with RCA and with news that he was set to work on his third album.

He also played his first gig in Vietnam on January 4.

On January 31, meanwhile, he performed at the Hammerstein Ballroom in NYC as part of the We Are Family Foundation charity event. He performed 'Shady' with Sam Sparro and Nile Rodgers who co-wrote it with Lambert. It was the first time the song, which feature son his second opus, was performed live.

Lambert spoke to Ryan Seacrest about the collaboration with Chic's Nile Rodgers: "I had gone to a friend's birthday party the night before and had been talking to Nile that week ... and he calls me the next morning and says, 'Hey Adam, I'm down here in the studio. You should come down here.' And I was like, 'Shoot! I didn't know, I went out last night ... Dude, I had a really good time at this party ... I don't think you're going to want me there.' And he's like, 'Just come down!'"

He continued: "So I get down to the studio and he has a chorus worked out and the first line of the verse and he's like, 'What do you think?' And I was like, 'Okay, do you want me to keep writing it?' So we just did it in about 35 minutes and I recorded it and it was done. On the spot, it was done...I got a demo back, and was like, 'Should I go back in and record it for real?' And they were like, 'No, we love it!'"

As for working with Sparro, he told celebrity gossip writer Dean Piper: "He's the coolest guy. He's so funny. He's got great fashion sense. We cackle every time we get together to write. He's so damn funny. Shady is just us. It's goofy and us being us. The lyrics are very out there. I think 'Shady' will be the underground video hit on *Trespassing*. It's a funny jam about 'cruising' basically. Or going out and getting into trouble and being nasty. No matter what background you're in everybody likes getting shady now and again."

The We Are Glamily Tour commenced on February 17 in Seoul and consisted of seventeen dates in Asia and Europe. Lambert had recently seen Prince in concert and it shift his perception of what a live concert can – and should – be. Lambert is a huge fan of pop music from Lady Gaga to Katy Perry by the way of Britney Spears, Madonna and even Justin Timberlake but he also loves classic rock music and funk. His idea for the tour was to combine pop with rock – with lots of makeup and snazzy costumes.

Performing live is made very safe and comfortable because of his devoted fanbase who are very enthusiastic and accepting. It's like a family, they are there for each other and it's a safe place for him.

He opened with a version of Rhianna's 'Stay' during the Asian leg of the tour. The online videos, of which, received rave reviews from fans and music critics. Some rehearsal footage of the opening night of the tour was made available online. "It was a preview! It was rehearsal. More to come!" He later tweeted after the gig: "Thank u Tokyo for an amazing run!"

Lambert speaking to Arnold Wayne Jones of the *Dallas Voice*: "I think that any sort of diehard fandom is a crazy, surreal mentality. That's part of the fun for the Glamberts; they've given themselves permission within that community to be kind of insane. And it's gorgeous and it's fun and it's an escape. It's not real life – it's something else. Everybody wants that in some form or another. We all have our different versions of it. For people who are diehard fans, that's their way, that's their obsession and that's their outlet."

As far as the setlist and stage production went, Lambert did not plan too far ahead. He's a fairly impulsive person, as he told *Today Online*'s Farah Daley: "we rehearsed this basic set featuring music from the two albums, figuring out a flow that made sense. We get to sound check on the day of the show and maybe one song we take out and we've been working in new songs here and there; covers and other surprises. Same thing with the outfits, I've got two big suitcases of clothes that I brought and I'll point 'I'll wear that at this part, that at this part and that at this part.' It makes it more fun and spontaneous. There might be some new song, there might not be, I don't know."

An example of one of his setlists looked like this: "If I Had

You', 'Naked Love', 'Cuckoo Play', 'Never Close Our Eyes', 'Pop That Lock', 'Chokehold', 'Shout' (Tears For Fears cover), 'Whataya Want From Me', 'Is This Love' (Bob Marley & The Wailers cover), 'Outlaws Of Love', 'Fever', 'For Your Entertainment', 'Dragon Attack' (Queen cover) and 'Shady' with an encore of 'Music Again' and 'Trespassing'.

He performed his first solo gig in Honk Kong on March 5 and performed in Singapore on March 8, however it was given an 'Advisory Of 16 An Above' label by the Media Development Authority after complaints that it promoted a gay lifestyle.

A piece of good news came his way when he was named as the official spokesperson for the Chinese release of the Trion video game *Rift*.

On March 15 he performed in Belarus though controversy followed him in Russia after the anti-homosexual laws raised the age of entry to 18 at his St. Petersburg show and an official security alert was given to US citizens intending to go to the show.

The tour finished on March 22 in Helsinki.

Lambert continued to spend time in East Asia after he won the 'Favorite International Artist' award at the STAR TV 17th Chinese Music awards in Macau in April. He sang two songs from his second album which was seen by an estimated two billion people. In Shanghai he appeared on Dragon TV's 80's *TalkShow* which included performances of 'Pop That Lock' from *Trespassing* and 'Mad World'. He also appeared on *Chinese Idol* as a guest judge.

Lambert bagged the award for 'Outstanding Music Artist' at the 24th GLAAD Media Awards on May 11 before he made another return to *American Idol* on May 16 where he performed a duet ('Titanium') with Angie Miller, a finalist in the Top 3.

A letter was sent to *The Hollywood Reporter* on July 12 which stated that Lambert was leaving RCA after the label reportedly planned a covers album when Lambert was already working on original material for his third full-length studio release. Rumours circulated that Lambert was going to collaborate with Nile Rodgers and DJ-producer Avicii after they appeared onstage together at a Long Island benefit show in August. They performed 'Lay Me Down' from Avicii's debut album *TRUE*.

Lambert has always felt it important to dedicate as much of his spare time as possible to charitable causes especially in the gay community.

"I'm a celebrity because of what I do," Lambert explained to *Details* in 2014, "my talent, I think, that's first and foremost, but as an out celebrity I have this great opportunity to try and influence people, or open their minds, or give them strength, in both the gay community or the mainstream straight community. I just think it's exciting to be able to be in that position, and so I always try to have something going on, and yeah, I think if it feels right, I go with that one."

However, Lambert collaborated again with Queen on September 20 2013 on the closing night of the iHeartRadio Music Festival at Las Vegas' MGM Grand Arena. The festival was broadcast live on Clear Channel to 150 US markets.

Speaking to *Kings Of A&R* in 2011, guitarist and friend Monte Pittman enthused: "He recently played with Queen and I thought it was brilliant. It's a phenomenal experience seeing a friend achieve so much so quickly. He's really defined in what he wants and can be a perfectionist about it. You can hear for yourself when you hear him sing. I think he's out of everyone's league on that show."

The critics praised Q+AL's performance in Sin City.

Steve Baltin of *Grammy.com* enthused: "So much of the reason why this incarnation of Queen is exciting is Lambert, whose confidence and theatricality fit like a glove. While his admiration of Mercury is clear to see, he is wisely not trying to replace an irreplaceable legend. Of course, May and drummer Roger Taylor remain two of rock's finest at their respective instruments and they propel this version of Queen to lofty standards. That pedigree came through especially on the rock grandeur of 'Fat Bottomed Girls', but also on the musically bipolar 'Under Pressure', Queen's classic duet with David Bowie, which excelled with Taylor handling a majority of the vocals."

Hollywood Reporter's Shirley Halperin wrote: "Decked all in black and donning a pair of stylish, silvery platform shoes (presumably Louboutins, judging from their cherry red soles), Lambert sported a mustache that would have made the late Freddie Mercury proud. With the perfect mix of rock attitude mixed with style, theatricality, sex appeal and impressive vocal gymnastics, he took the band's music to new heights in front of a worldwide audience."

Billboard's Jason Lipshutz wrote: "With each new show,

Lambert's involvement with the five-decade-old band makes more sense: Freddie Mercury's king-sized songwriting makes for a perfect vessel for Lambert's operatic wail, and iHeartRadio fest attendees who wanted to stick around for 'Another One Bites The Dust' got to witness the magnetic power of Lambert's pristine high notes. The former *American Idol* runner-up oozed charisma as he strutted around the stage, winking at his reputation of a fill-in while also reminding people they should still pay attention to his solo career whenever this stint with Queen, er, bites the dust."

They played an eight song setlist: 'We Will Rock You', 'Another One Bites The Dust', 'Crazy Little Thing Called Love', 'Love Kills', 'Fat Bottomed Girls', 'Under Pressure', 'We Are The Champions' and 'Don't Stop Me Now'.

Lambert made his debut on the popular TV high school musical *Glee* which was announced in July by the show's co-creator Ryan Murphy. The episode titled 'A Katy Or A Gaga' aired on Fox on November 7. Lambert played Elliot 'Starchild' Gilbert and performed a version of Lady Gaga's 'Marry The Night' (which was released before the episode's air date) climbed to Number 39 on the Pop Digital Songs chart the week after the episode was shown on TV.

"It's such a good episode," Lambert said to US presenter Ryan Seacrest. "I've had such a good time with everybody. The cast, they're a big family and they're super tight-knit and have a bunch of inside jokes, but they welcomed me with open arms." He went on to say that he sees much of himself in his character: "He goes into this audition and he gives them everything he has … he wears this obnoxious costume … and I think he's just a dreamer and he gets up there and Kurt gets a bit threatened and says, 'It's not for me.'"

2013 ended on a high after Lambert received the 'Best International Male Vocalist' and 'Fan Choice Award' on December 18 at China's Huading Music Awards ceremony. He played a few more concerts before the year closed, including 'Lay Me Down' at the Hard Rock Hotel and Casino. He was named by *Forbes* as one of the top earning *American Idols* of the year.

While 2013 may have been a tremendous year in a professional sense but it also brought an end to his relationship with Sauli Koskinen. The pair were arrested outside a bar in Helsinki in December. Needless to say, the incident was featured heavily in the celebrity press.

Lambert spoke to *The Hot Hits* about that evening: "I walked away from the situation and realised, you know, my boyfriend and I are cool, everything is fine. And we said ok, let's take responsibility for our actions here, look at ourselves in the mirror and work together as a team to maybe turn a negative into a positive."

He added: "We looked at it and I said A, I want to take more responsibility for my actions and not act like a child like I did that night, and B just change my lifestyle a little bit."

The relationship had been on its way out for a couple of months leading up to its eventual split. With Lambert travelling so much and Koskinen working on Finnish TV they just couldn't find the time to be together as much as they would have liked. Things had just ran their course between them and it was time to move on separately.

"Fame is not easy. Celebrities are only human. Love is not easy either, but it is forever!" Koskinen wrote in a blog post.

Lambert on the other hand wrote about it with humour on Twitter: "Jetlag+Vodka=blackout. Us÷blackout=irrational confusion. jail+guilt+press=lesson learned. Sauli+Adam+hangover burgers= laughing bout it."

Lambert chose to dedicate himself to his work. Music came first.

Another one of Lambert's passions is fashion. He is a very visual artist – he loves the hair, make-up and clothes. He's very much like a New Romantic from the 1980s; a Boy George or Steve Stranger type pop star.

"When I read a magazine and see an editorial I remember it and sometimes I'll just take my phone out and take pictures of what I see," he said to Farah Daley of *Today Online*. "I love high-fashion; I love the stuff that they're doing on the runways. I also like things that are completely left field that aren't necessarily totally chic, something that's totally weird. I don't take fashion too seriously in the sense that I get ridiculous sometimes. Sometimes I look crazy and that's part of my expression: that I want to let go and be expressive and maybe inspire the sense of a smile in somebody."

His life had changed immeasurably since *Idol*. He was doing a lot of theatre work and interested in recording and performing his own music and while he thought he could have had a bit more time to refine his talents *Idol* had helped him become a successful pop star. He had achieved his dreams. *Idol* gave him the platform for TV and for industry contacts which he might not otherwise have had. However, there is always a stigma attached to any *Idol* contestant, either the runner ups or the winner. Certainly not everyone who enters and success, to an extent, in a TV talent contest is lucky to launch a career. Kelly Clarkson is an example of a success story.

In terms of his image and sound he has developed significantly since his *Idol* days, as he explained to Lina Lecaro of *LA Slush*: "And as the kid from *America Idol*. Those two things I kind of wanted to flip. A lot of the funk stuff, there's guitar in it, and funk comes from rock, but there's a lot of R&B feel. Like Michael and Prince, a lot of energy… A lot of stuff I loved to listen to. When I was on *Idol*, I think I was drawn to singing rock music because, a) the type of range I have was the type of range that felt right for rock songs… male rock songs that I could show my range on. And b) because there was no "rock" performer on the show, so that was my thing."

Living in LA since he was 19, Lambert was used to the

hustle and bustle of city life and now he was a celebrity he was getting used to being approached in the street for his autograph or picture. He's friendly with people if they are cool with him and they're just chatting and exchanging stories and such but if they're rude and upset his friends or family he'll be less inclined to help out. He's well away that some people just want a picture for their Facebook profile. It's the modern world of social networking.

"If we're talking in a club and we're at a club and you're like, 'it'd be really cool for me to get a picture with you,'" Lambert explained to Lina Lecaro of *LA Slush*. "I don't give a shit, but when you're trying to work me... It's really a case by case thing, it's the energy of the person. It has nothing to do with the act or what's being said, it's how it's being presented and that's life. Like being picked up at a bar – if someone says a cheesy line but they're really cute and funny about it, and they're making eye contact and they're genuine, it's like 'You just gave me a line.'"

Adam Lambert was now a modern pop icon, he had gone from a TV show talent contest to a fully-fledge pop star with two albums and two solo headlining tours under his belt. He had also fronted one of the world's most loved rock bands. Not only does his music have an impact on people, but his likeable, friendly personality makes him seem approachable and the media love him for it, even though they focus far more than they should on his sexuality. As he has said himself, repeatedly, it should be about the music and the performances. But that's celebrity gossip for ya. As for fronting Queen in 2012, that was only the beginning.

2014 would be the biggest year of his professional career to date.

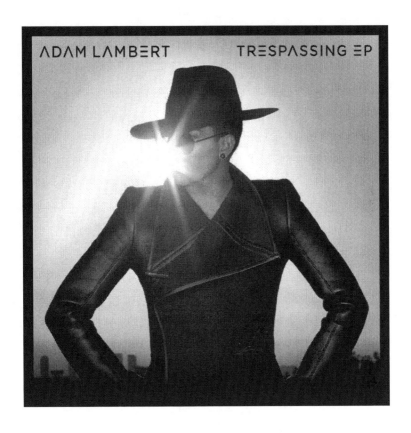

FRONTING QUEEN

"His voice is second to none," *Idol* creator Simon Fuller commented to Nancy Jo Sales of *Details* in 2009. "It's up there with the all-time great singers I've come across. Many millions of people have already fallen in love with him. He's got that glint in his eye, whether you're gay, whatever, it's just attractive. He's just a very sexual guy – and he's not threatening to women."

2014 kicked off with appearances in *American Idol* and *RuPaul's Drag Race*, the Logo TV reality show. He also returned to *Glee* in an episode called 'Frenemies' which aired on February 25. Lambert performed The Darkness' 'I Believe In A Thing Called Love'; he then returned in the following week's episode 'Trio' where he sang a cover of Heart's classic track, 'Barracuda'. His final appearance on *Glee* aired on April 1 with a rendition of A Great Big World's 'Rockstar'.

May 27 saw the release of *The Very Best Of Adam Lambert* as part of the Sony Legacy Playlist series. It features songs culled from his first two solo albums as well as recordings from *American Idol* and *Glee*. It debuted at Number 14 on the *Billboard* Top Internet Albums chart.

The tracklisting features 'Mad World', 'One', 'Tracks Of My Tears', 'Time For Miracles', 'For Your Entertainment', 'Whataya Want From Me', 'If I Had You', 'Aftermath', 'Can't Let You Go', 'Trespassing', 'Never Close Our Eyes', 'Better Than I Know Myself', 'Runnin'' and 'Marry The Night' (*Glee* version).

It was announced on March 6 that a full scale North American Queen + Adam Lambert tour was taking place with 19 initial dates beginning in Chicago on June 19. It was announced on *Good Morning America* and at a press conference at Madison Square Garden. Lambert confirmed on March 15 that the Madison Square Garden gig had sold out in a day and that five extra shows had been added due to overwhelming demand.

Everything went well at the production rehearsals in London where they arranged the setlist and rehearsed for the tour. They geared the set towards the die-hard Queen fans and the more causal fans, so all the big hits are in the setlist as well as some lesser known tunes such as 'In The Lap Of The Gods' and 'Stone Cold Crazy'. One song they decided to adopt for the US setlist was 'Love Kills', a 1984 Freddie Mercury track that was recorded with

Giorgio Moroder for the remastered and restored version of Fritz Lang's 1927 silent sci-fi masterpiece, *Metropolis*. They took out the disco element and made it more of a traditional Queen song, which is included on the recent compilation *Queen Forever*. It was an exciting albeit nerve-wrecking period for Lambert. To go from auditioning for *American Idol* back in 2009 with 'Bohemian Rhapsody' to actually fronting Queen is an unbelievable journey.

The one thing Lambert wanted to stress was that he is in by no means replacing Mercury. He knew enough and is talented enough to both honour Mercury yet add his own style to the songs.

"I remember seeing some footage of him and thinking, 'Wow, this guy is on fire! What an amazing performer!'" he said to the *Advocate*'s Daniel Reynolds in 2014.

Entertainment Weekly's Erika Berlin raved over the band's performance at the sold out Madison Square Garden gig: "So while his skinny leather pants, leopard-print tuxes, and use of studs and fringe in a single outfit would likely all be Freddie-approved, Adam Lambert was very much his glam-punk self, and Mercury still kept a couple of coveted solos for himself."

Also reviewing said Madison Square Garden gig, *New York Daily News*' Kevin Coughlin: "Last, but certainly not the least, former *American Idol* finalist Adam Lambert channels the spirit of Queen's late frontman Freddie Mercury in almost every detail. Strutting the curvaceous stage like a black leather-clad peacock with a slight pompadour, Lambert launched into the set opener, 'Now I'm Here' with ferocity and vigour. At times, Lambert's presence appeared to rejuvenate and energize May's and Taylor's performance throughout the 2 hour 15-minute, 23-song set."

They were also set to play at The Forum in Los Angeles where the band had last performed in 1982.

"It's a great place to be; I feel so fortunate to be going out there. I never thought it would happen again," May explained to Eddie Trunk on *That Metal Show*. "When Freddie went, I thought: 'That's it. We did that. It was a great life. Now, it's time to have a different life.' And for years, we didn't try to be Queen in any way. I would look at the Forum in LA, and I would look at Madison Square Garden, and I would think: 'Those were the days.' To come back now, all of these years later, and to fill those places and to hear that noise. That's vindication for the fact that we should be playing, we should be out there. I feel overcome with it, really."

Having retired from the music scene Queen bassist John Deacon declined to take part, having not been directly involved with the band since 1997. Joining May, Taylor and Lambert was long-time keyboardist Spike Edney, bassist Neil Fairclough and percussionist Rufus Tiger Taylor (Roger Taylor's son).

"After we lost Freddie, there was a long period for Roger and I where we didn't want to talk about it," May admitted to *Planet Rock*'s Nicky Horne. "That was a part of our lives that we had done, and now we were individuals. But it comes back, because people actually do want to hear the music. We're still able to play, and we can bring Freddie back and we can bring John back – even though neither of them are with us on stage, technically. Spiritually, they are."

They took the tour around the world when they headlined Korea's Super Sonic 2014 festival in Seoul in August (Queen had never played Korea) and Japan's Summer Sonic 2014 festival in Osaka and Tokyo on August 16 and 17 where they had last performed eight years previously with Paul Rodgers.

After thirty years, Queen were set to return to Australia for the first time since 1985 after a tour was announced in May. The band announced an initial four dates with a further two shows added due to demand. It kicked off in Perth on August 22 and shows were staged in Sydney, Melbourne and Brisbane on September 1. Shows were also staged in New Zealand at Auckland's Vector Arena from September 3 to 4.

Daily Review's Ben Neutze reviewed one of the Sydney shows at the Allphones Arena: "When pop icon of the moment Lady Gaga (who took her name from the band's 1984 hit 'Radio Ga Ga') appeared onstage as a surprise guest to duet with Lambert on 'Another One Bites The Dust', we caught a glimpse of a similar kind of raw, unpredictable power, as she strutted and fidgeted around the stage and down the catwalk in an obnoxiously large black wig and skin-tight velvet bodysuit."

Noise 101's Paul Cashmere reviewed the band's visit to Melbourne on August 30 and wrote: "Adam Lambert does not try to replace Freddie Mercury, or invent the songs. He plays a humble alternative delivering these classics as they were originally intended."

The 35 date tour was a huge critical and commercial success. The North American and Oceania tour, according to Pollstar, grossed $37 million and was ranked 35th in the Top 100 worldwide tours of 2014.

Roger Taylor raved about Lambert to *Ultimate Classic Rock*'s Matt Wardlaw: "I have to say, it was just great. You know, we got on so well with Adam. He fitted in so well with us and he brought so much to the show. [He's a] great frontman and he looked great and he sings beautifully, and his style is very suited to our music. You know, it's pretty theatrical music, some of our stuff. He's the greatest. So, we really had a ball and I think it came over in the shows. They were very well attended and the reception that we got in every city was great. So, it was a really great experience and I'm thrilled."

There's certainly a difference between singing Queen songs, many of which are universally well-known and without much effort encourage the audience to sing along and dance while his own solo work requires more work when involving the audience.

"It's a huge challenge as well, because there's been a lot of expectation and doubt," he said to the *Advocate*'s Daniel Reynolds in 2014. "You have a mix of people in the audience that are diehard Queen fans, and I have my fans that are coming to the show kind of through me. It's interesting bringing them all together and seeing how it all plays out."

The 2014 setlist looked like this 'Procession' (recorded intro), 'Now I'm Here', 'Stone Cold Crazy', 'Another One Bites The Dust', 'Fat Bottomed Girls', 'In The Lap Of The Gods…Revisited', 'Seven Seas Of Rhye', 'Killer Queen', 'Somebody To Love', 'I Want It All', 'Love Of My Life', ''39', 'These Are The Days Of Our Lives', (bass solo / drum battle) 'Under Pressure', 'Love Kills', 'Who Wants To Live Forever', (guitar solo) 'Last Horizon', 'Tie Your Mother Down', 'Radio Ga Ga' 'Crazy Little Thing Called Love', 'The Show Must Go On' and 'Bohemian Rhapsody' with an encore of 'We Will Rock You' and 'We Are The Champions' and the closing tape of 'God Save The Queen'.

Some shows featured ;'Don't Stop Me Now' in place of 'Radio Ga Ga' and 'Dragon Attack' instead of 'Love Kills'. They also played 'I Was Born To Love You' in Japan and even the Brian May penned 'Tea Torriatte'.

May told Japan's Universal Music: "They're difficult songs to sing, Queen songs. There's too much range. So many people can't sing them in the original key – even if they are good singers, Adam comes along, [and] he can do it easy. He can do it in his sleep! He can sing higher than even Freddie could in a live situation. So I think Freddie would look at this guy and think, 'Hmm... Yeah. Okay.' There would be a kind of, 'Hmm ... You bastard. You can do this.'"

After the tour came to an end he resumed work on his next solo opus.

"I think there will be, yeah. I'm working with an amazing executive producer," he said to Ryan Seacrest in September. "Again, I can't say too much, but it's gonna be really good."

On September 19 an initial 21 date UK and Europe tour for was announced that was set to cover ten countries beginning in January 2015. A second O2 show in London was added as other dates in the UK such as Liverpool due to overwhelming demand for tickets. The tour ventured to an eleventh country after it was announced they were set to play Krakow Arena in Poland bringing the tour to 26 dates. The 10th annual *Classic Rock* Roll Of Honours Awards named Queen + Adam Lambert the 'Band Of The Year' on November 4.

The band made an appearance performing 'I Want It All'

and 'Who Wants To Live Forever' on Helene Fischer's annual Christmas show on December 24 on Berlin before a performance of 'Somebody To Love' with contestants on the UK's *The X Factor*.

The *Daily Mirror*'s Sophia Rahman wrote about the band's appearance on the popular talent show: "Ageing rockers Queen and their quiffed singer Adam Lambert joined the contestants to open tonight's nail-biting show with a rousing performance of their classic 'Somebody To Love'. Judges Mel B, Cheryl, Simon and Louis gave a standing ovation to the foursome and Adam had some advice for the wannabe popstars. The be-quiffed singer told Dermot the hopefuls should 'be present in every moment and think ahead'."

It was announced that they were to play an exclusive New Year's Eve gig at London's Central Hall Westminster next to Big Ben to bring in the New Year. It was broadcast on BBC one and staged by BBC Music. The event was dubbed 'Queen + Adam Lambert Rock Big Ben Live' and was broadcast live from 23:15 to 00:30 with a pause between 23:59 to 00:10 to celebrate the New Year with a fireworks display above the River Thames.

The first part of the gig was seen by an average of 5.83

million people while the second part was seen by an estimated 10 million viewers. It was streamed live on BBC music and presented by presented by BBC Radio 1 DJ's Greg James and Gemma Cairney.

The setlist featured 'Don't Stop Me Now', 'I Want To Break Free', 'Somebody To Love', 'Another One Bites The Dust', 'Under Pressure', 'Fat Bottomed Girls', 'Radio Ga Ga', 'I Want It All', 'Crazy Little Thing Called Love' and 'The Show Must Go On' with an encore of 'Bohemian Rhapsody' and 'Killer Queen' (medley) and 'We Will Rock You' and 'We Are The Champions'.

A recording of Freddie Mercury from *Rock Montreal* was shown during 'Bohemian Rhapsody' and the start of 'We Will Rock You' featured bagpipes.

The concert brought Lambert to the forefront of the UK public after it was announced he came up tops in the Goggle Trends searching list.

"It's not, in any sense, a copy," May told *Planet Rock*'s Nicky Horne of the Queen + Adam Lambert shows. "And it's a joy for me to explore this material with Adam. The final piece of the jigsaw puzzle is that he's a nice guy. If he was a shit, it wouldn't have been fun – and it wouldn't have happened. [Laughs.] He's a good guy, he's fun, he entertaining and he's open to ideas. And he bring lots of ideas in, so when we were putting this setlist together he didn't just go, 'OK, I'll do what you want.' He said, 'How about we try this? 'Let's do this.' So, we had a real proper birth process. It's great. I just feel very grateful, Nicky."

Queen + Adam Lambert appeared on the cover *Classic Rock* magazine in January.

On January 15, Lambert appeared as guest judge, the first former contestant to do so, on the fourteenth season of *American Idol* during the NYC auditions filling in for Keith Urban alongside fellow judges Jennifer Lopez and Harry Connick, Jr.

Lambert then revealed in an interview with *Billboard* that he had signed to Warner Bros. Records within twenty-four hours of leaving RCA. He also stated that his third album was set for an early summer release with a single due in April which was to be executive produced by Swedish singer-producers Max Martin and Shellback. It was written in Sweden in early 2014. The title of the album was announced on January 29, 2015 and titled *The Original High*.

"I'm not finished with that," he said to *Rolling Stone*'s Andy Greene back in 2014 about his third solo opus. Finding the time amongst his other creative pursuits and the Queen tour was demanding. "I've done a lot of work and there's some amazing music. We'd probably be able to put something out now, but I'm a perfectionist and I have to make sure that I love every song 100 percent and that they're perfect for me. I maybe want to find even more material. I'm not going to rush a project like this."

With his third album on the way, he hoped to eclipse the success of *Trespassing* and continue to make a dent in today's saturated but mostly uninspiring pop world. Part of what he does is to inspire people. He goes through periods of self-worth and doubt just like anyone else even if he doesn't through it onstage, which is often just a facade; it's like acting. He's built up confidence over the years and has become more comfortable with himself. He's learned a lot from past relationships, friends, family and colleagues.

The Queen tour in the UK and Europe, meanwhile, was going down a storm receiving rave reviews from fans and critics.

May praised Lambert's showmanship in an interview with Japan's Universal Music: "He doesn't have to try. He is a natural, in the same way that Freddie was…We didn't look for this guy, [but] suddenly he's there, and he can sing all of those lines... He doesn't imitate; he just does his own thing."

The 2015 setlist ran as follows: 'One Vision', 'Stone Cold Crazy', 'Another One Bites The Dust', 'Fat Bottomed Girls', 'In The Lap Of The Gods…Revisited', 'Seven Seas Of Rhye', 'Killer Queen', 'I Want To Break Free', 'Don't Stop Me Now', 'Somebody To Love', 'Love Of My Life', ''39', 'These Are The Days Of Our Lives' (bass solo / drum battle) 'Under Pressure', 'Save Me', 'Who Wants To Live Forever', (guitar solo) 'Last Horizon', 'Tie Your Mother Down', 'I Want It All', 'Radio Ga Ga', 'Crazy Little Thing Called Love' and 'Bohemian Rhapsody' with an encore of 'We Will Rock You' and 'We Are The Champions' followed by a recording of 'God Save The Queen to close the show.

Some shows had 'A Kind Of Magic' in replace of 'These Are The Days Of Our Lives' and an addition of 'the Show Must Go On'.

Catherine Gee of *The Daily Telegraph* gave the band's performance at London's O2 Arena on January 17 4/5 and enthused: "At the time, Adam Lambert was just three years old.

But it's his youth and rapturous energy that has given Queen the glittering boost that they've been so desperately lacking since Mercury's death. Without attempting to impersonate Mercury – if anything, he looks more like George Michael – Lambert has brought dazzling showmanship and style back to the band. He's also everything that Queen's last long-term singer, the blokey, bluesy, ex-Bad Company frontman Paul Rodgers, is not."

The Guardian's Dave Simpson said of the tour's opening night in Newcastle: "When Lambert claps hands, the audience clap with him, unprompted. His unusually wide vocal range allows him to hit high notes (notably Mercury's famous one in 'Somebody To Love') which would normally require the assistance of even tighter trousers."

He continued: "However, the Indianan is no mere talent show get-lucky. Like Mercury, Lambert paid his dues with opera training, theatre, singing in clubs and performing dance and rock, which has given him the dexterity to tackle a catalogue stretching from thumping grooves ('Radio Ga Ga', 'Another One Bites The Dust') to blistering hard rock ('Seven Seas of Rhye', 'Tie Your Mother Down')."

In Manchester, Katie Fitzpatrick of the *Manchester Evening News* raved: "He isn't meant to be a Freddie clone. But here is a charismatic singer who performs and celebrates Queen's timeless back catalogue, including 'Another One Bites The Dust', 'Tie Your Mother Down' and 'Fat Bottomed Girls', exactly the way they should be with added new electricity."

In Leeds, the *Daily Express'* Paul Jeeves wrote: "Every song is a nailed-on humdinger of a classic and yet it is this, and the lack of odd curveball or rarity, that perhaps creates the West End vibe of the concert. In many ways this is the ultimate homage to Queen and with that in mind, Lambert is as good as it is going to get for fans who yearn for the impossible. And when the song is right boy can this fella sing. He holds all the notes in all the right places and his range is more than impressive. 'I Want It All', 'Radio GaGa', 'Crazy Little Thing Called Love' all fit Lambert's vocals like a glove and as the crowd embraces him his charisma shines through."

However, the band were forced to cancel the planned Brussels show after Lambert was diagnosed with severe bronchitis and was ordered 24 hour vocal and bed rest by a doctor. Because of the unavailability of the venue they were unable to reschedule and so the show had to be axed entirely. He tweeted: "Thanks for the well wishes guys! Send me some healing energy, I'll drink a ton of water and sleep! Sound like a plan?" and "Brussels: sad we had to cancel tonight. The last thing I'd want is to let u down but I'm under doctors orders to stay in bed and get well. Thank you for your understanding and patience. ;)"

Q+AL brought an end to their sold-out European tour at Sheffield Motorpoint Arena on Feb 27. However it did not prove to be the end of the collaboration. A press release was published on February 27, part of which read: "Following 67 sold-out concerts performed together around the world, Queen + Adam Lambert head to South America to top the opening night at Rock in Rio Brazil '30 Years Celebration' edition on Friday September 18."

And continued: "Rio de Janeiro, February, 26th, 2015 – Says Rock in Rio President and Founder Roberto Medina: '30 years ago, Queen performed in front of 250,000 people who fell in love with the band, and it became one of the most iconic moments of Rock in Rio. I am positive that the moments from 30 years ago will be rejuvenated and rejoiced with Queen + Adam Lambert, making it again a moment no one will ever forget.'"

What an incredible opportunity for both Adam Lambert and Queen.

Q+AL have not announced plans for any more shows the release of their first live album and DVD but they have suggested the possibility of some new studio material.

"It really is a dream job, and it's really cool," he enthused to Matthew Breen of the *Advocate* in 2011. "I do stop and keep it all in perspective. This is pop music, and it's not fucking brain surgery. I mean, some of it's serious…but some of it's just really fun dance music. And I'm wearing eight pounds of makeup because I fucking want to. Why not?"

There's a fine balancing act between artistic creativity and freedom and making money and selling records. Artists have to make a living too. It took time for Lambert to figure out the business but he remains surrounded by good people who keep him grounded and whose advice he respects.

Lambert has learned how to deal with fame and life in the spotlight.

"I just kind of got a little stressed out, and I was taking it all very seriously and getting really nitpicky about things. I was really beating myself up about performances and how I looked and this and that," he explained to Oprah Winfrey on her show in 2010. "As the year came to an end, [I realized] this is a once-in-a-lifetime opportunity. I need to enjoy this. This is amazing. I got what I wanted."

He also learned a spot of advice from Madonna when he met her at her NYC apartment.

"I said, 'I'm sorry, I'm sorry. I'm just really intimidated right now.' And she said, 'Why?' " he said to Oprah Winfrey. "'Because I love you!' And she said, 'So love equals intimidation for you?' And I said, 'Yes, pretty much. Most of the time, I think, when I feel love, that's the way it manifests itself at first.'… [She said], 'Just keep your eye on the prize and put your blinders up.'" Lambert added: "'Don't get sidetracked with all the extra fuss.'"

Lambert attended the Brit awards in London in February after the band's sold out Wembley Arena show. He mentioned that he would love to work with UK singers Ed Sheeran and Sam Smith. "There's a lot of great singers here tonight. The UK is pumping out incredible vocalists," he said to *Mirror Celebs*. And added: "If there's a popular singer right now, it's probably coming out of here."

He briefly spoke about *The Original High* but didn't divulge too much information other than that it is an electronic and dance based album due in the summer. "I have some collaborations but I can't really talk about them yet unfortunately," he told *Mirror Celebs*.

With a third album due in 2015 and at the time of writing the Q+AL European tour has come to an end with rave reviews and strong ticket sales it looks as though the year will be an excellent one for the former *Idol* contestant.

Photos by Chris Mee, 2015

Photos by Chris Mee, 2015

Photos by Chris Mee, 2015

Photos by Chris Mee, 2015

Photos by Chris Mee, 2015

Photos by Chris Mee, 2015

Photos by Chris Mee, 2015

Photos by Chris Mee, 2015

Photos by Chris Mee, 2015

Photos by Chris Mee, 2015

Photos by Chris Mee, 2015

Photos by Chris Mee, 2015

PART TWO

TIMELINE

Here's a list of some of the most important dates in Adam Lambert's life and career; wherever possible exact date shave been given...

1982

January 29 – Adam Lambert was born in Indianapolis

2009

May 8 – San Diego Mayor Jerry Sanders declared 'Adam Lambert Day'

May 20 – 'No Boundaries' was released digitally

May – Lambert appeared on the cover of *Entertainment Weekly*

June – Lambert appeared on the cover of *Rolling Stone*

June 30 – *Season 8 Favorite Performances* was released digitally

July 5 – The first date of the American Idols LIVE! Tour

September 15 – The final night of the American Idols LIVE! Tour

October 18 – 'Time For Miracles' was released

October 27 – 'For Your Entertainment' was released

November 17 – *Take One* was released

November 22 – Lambert performed 'For Your Entertainment' on the American Music Awards Of 2009

November 23 – *For Your Entertainment* was released

November 24 – 'Whataya Want From Me' was released

November – Lambert appeared on the cover of *Details*

December – Lambert hosted and performed at Jingle Balls in New York, Miami and Tampa

2010

February – Lambert played a five song AOL Sessions concert

April 9 – *Remixes* was released digitally

April – Lambert returned to *American Idol* as a guest

May 11 – 'If I Had You' was released

May – Lambert appeared on the cover of Japan's *Rolling Stone*

June 4 – Lambert kicked off the Glam Nation Tour

June – Lambert appeared at MuchMusic Awards in Canada

June – Teamed up with 'Glam A Classroom' campaign

September 17 – 'Fever' was released digitally

October – Collaborated with The Pennyroyal Studio on a second Signature Collection

November – Started dating Finnish TV personality Sauli Koskinen

December 6 – *Acoustic Live!* was released

December 16 – The final night of the Glam Nation Tour

2011

January 24 – 'Sure Fire Winners' was released digitally

January – Lambert signed a worldwide music publishing deal with Kobalt Music Group

March 8 – 'Aftermath' was released digitally

March 10 – Returned to *American Idol*

March 22 – *Glam Nation Live* was released

March 25 – 'Sleepwalker' was released

August – Lambert was the subject of an episode of VH-1's *Behind The Music*

August – Lambert signed to Direct Management Group

August – Presented the 'Equality Idol Award' by Sam Sparro at the Equality California Los Angeles Equality Awards

October 18 – *Beg For Mercy* was released

November – Lambert joined Queen at the MTV Europe Music Awards

December 20 – 'Better Than I Know Myself' was released

December – Queen drummer Roger Taylor confirmed that they were in talks with Lambert for some more live shows

2012

April 14 – 'Never Close Our Eyes' was released digitally

May 15 – *Trespassing* was released

May 17 – Appeared on *American Idol*

June 7 – Lambert appeared at the Rays Of Sunshine Children's Charity at London's Royal Albert Hall

June 30 – Performed with Queen in the Ukraine in the first of six live dates

July 11-14 – Three Q+AL dates in London at the Hammersmith Apollo; last shows together of 2012

September 25 – Headlined a benefit concert, Marylanders for Marriage Equality, in Washington, D.C.

October 8 – 'Trespassing' was released digitally

October 16 – *Trespassing EP* was released

October – Appeared in a Halloween special of *Pretty Little Liars*

October – The *Sunday Mirror* reported that Lambert had insured his voice for $48 million

December 6 – Hosted and Performed at the VH-1 Divas concert

December – Appeared on the cover of *Fiasco*'s 'Obsession' special issue

December – Performed at 'Cyndi Lauper & Friends: Home For The Holidays' benefit concert

2013

January – Lambert announced that he would be leaving 19 Recordings but remain with RCA

January 31 – Performed Hammerstein Ballroom in New York City as part of the We Are Family Foundation charity concert

February 17 – First night of the We Are Glamily Tour in South Korea

March 22 – Final night of the We Are Glamily Tour in Helsinki

March – Lambert wrote an article for *Out* magazine's feature on David Bowie

April – Lambert announced his split from Finnish TV personality Sauli Koskinen

May 11 – Picked up the Outstanding Music Artist at the 24th GLAAD Media Awards

May 16 – Lambert returned to *American Idol* for the fourth time

May 25 – Performed at the opening ceremony of 2013 Life Ball in Vienna

May – Lambert was awarded the 'Hope Of Los Angeles Award'

June – 'Adam Lambert Day' was declared by the City Council of Pittsburgh

June 23 – Appeared at the Broadway Cares/Equity Fights AIDS benefit gig at Manhattan's Roseland Ballroom

July 12 – Sent a letter to The *Hollywood Reporter* stating that he planned to leave RCA Records

August 19 – Appeared at the All For The East End benefit gig in Long Island

September – Queen + Adam Lambert made the debut appearance in the US at the 2013 iHeartRadio Music Festival at the MGM Grand Arena, located on the Las Vegas Strip

September – Lambert topped Yahoo! Voices's poll of the 'Top 10 Pop Singers'

October 15 – Attended the premiere of the documentary movie *Bridgegroom* which he contributed a song to

November – Performed at South Florida's Make-A-Wish Foundation Ball

November 7 – His debut appeared on *Glee* aired

December 8 – Performed at TrevorLIVE gala, a fundraiser set up by The Trevor Project, at the Hollywood Palladium

December 18 – Appeared at China's Huading Music Awards where he bagged 'Best International Male Vocalist' and the 'Fan Choice Award'

2014

February – Returned to *American Idol* and appeared on *RuPaul's Drag Race* and *Glee*

February – He performed for the Family Equality Council's 10th Annual Los Angeles Award's dinner

March 6 – It was announced that Queen + Adam Lambert would tour the US and Canada

March – *Shades Of Elvis*, a photography book, was released featuring Lambert

May 27 – *The Very Best Of Adam Lambert* was released

June 19 – The first night of the Queen + Adam Lambert tour in Chicago

June – Lambert hooked up with AT&T for its second yearly 'Live Proud' campaign, in support of LGBT Pride Month and Pride season.

September 4 – The final night of the 2014 Q+AL tour in Auckland after visiting North America, South Korea, Japan, Australia and New Zealand

November 4 – Queen + Adam Lambert was named 'Band Of the Year' at the tenth annual *Classic Rock* Roll Of Honour Awards

December 25 – Q+AL appeared on Helene Fischer's annual Christmas show in Berlin

December 31 – Q+AL performed a special New Year's Eve gig at London Central Hall near Big Ben

2015

January 13 – Q+AL kicked off the UK and European tour in Newcastle

January 15 – Lambert appeared as a guest judge on *American Idol*

January 29 – Lambert revealed the title of his third solo album, *The Original High*

February 8 – Forced to cancel the Q+AL show in Brussels due to severe Bronchitis

February 27 – Final night of the European tour in Sheffield, UK

TRIVIA

Music fans love facts and bits of trivia so here are some tidbits of information about Adam Lambert.

Lambert is the first openly gay artist to achieve a Number 1 album on the *Billboard* album charts as well as the Digital Album Chart in both the US and Canada.

He received a Grammy Nomination for 'Best Male Pop Vocal Performance' in 2002 and an Honorary GLAAD Media Award in 2013.

The Times reported Lambert as the first openly gay artist to get a major US label deal.

By April 2012, his debut album sold close to two million copies and 4.2 million singles by January 2011.

Lambert's vocal range goes from bass E to B flat above tenor high C which gives him three octaves and six semitones.

The UK's *Sunday Times* reported in October 2012 that Lambert had insured his voice for $48 million.

Lambert came out top on Yahoo! Voices' list of Top 10 pop singers in September 2013.

Lambert is an enthusiastic follow of fashion and has appeared on MTV's *Talk@Playground* and Project Runway. He has appeared on many magazine covers such as the US magazine *Fault* in 2012 and the UK high style fashion magazine, Fiasco. He appeared at 2012's New York Fashion Week and as a guest on E!'s *Fashion Police*.

Lambert appeared in the photography book *Shades Of Elvis* by photographer Christopher Ameruoso and Priscilla Presley, released in March 2013.

Lambert's music is influenced by pop, classic rock, funk, disco, dubstep and electronic music with influences from David Bowie to Queen to Aerosmith, Led Zeppelin and Michael Jackson as well as Madonna.

Lambert is an avid philanthropist. Some of his charitable causes, contributions and associations include the 2010 'Glam A Classroom' campaign; various funds have been raised via DonorsChoose.org, MusiCares, The Trevor Project, Rays Of Sunshine Children's Charity, Olena Pinchuk ANTIAIDS Foundation, Marriage Equality, Family Equality Council, Gay Pride, We Are Family Foundation, Life Ball, Broadway Cares/Equity Fights AIDS, All For The East End (AFTEE), Make-A-Wish Foundation and UNICEF.

Lambert was handed the Hope Of Los Angeles Award in 2011.

Lambert is a role model for gay singers and artists and a champion for social justice. Lambert was presented with the 'Equality Idol Award' by Sam Sparro at the 2011 Equality California Los Angeles Equality Awards. He was also honored at the 2012 PFLAG National Los Angeles event. He was involved in the 2010 It Gets Better campaign against school bullying and the 2010 Spirit Day.

Lambert was a headliner at the 2012 Miami Beach Gay Pride Parade.

Lambert performed at the Cyndi Lauper & Friends: Home For The Holidays benefit gig which supported the True Colors Fund and its Forty To None Project which raises funds for homelessness in the LGBT (lesbian, gay, bisexual and transgender) youth.

The Adam Lambert Glambert Fan Army raised funds in 2011 for the MTV Dance Party Marathon in association with the National Bullying Prevention Month.

Lambert was involved in The New F Word campaign sponsored by the Friend Movement organization.

He headlined Pride In The Street in Pittsburgh in 2012.

Lambert contributed a song to the movie *Bridegroom*, a critically acclaimed documentary about marriage equality.

He has been on many TV shows such as *American Idol*, *Project Runway*, *Majors & Minors*, *Pretty Little Liars*, *VH-1 Divas*, *Glee* and *RuPaul's Drag Race*.

INFLUENCES

Here's a list of Adam Lambert's key musical influences...

AEROSMITH

By far one of the most universally successful American rock bands of all time, Aerosmith have sold over 150 million albums, almost half of which have been sold in the US alone. They regularly feature in polls of greatest bands and have been inducted into both the Rock And Roll Hall Of Fame and the Songwriters Hall Of Fame. The band is made up of singer Steven Tyler, guitarist Joe Perry and Brad Whitford, drummer Joey Kramer and bassist Tom Hamilton. Some of their famous albums include *Permanent Vacation* (1987), *Pump* (1989), *Get A Grip* (1993) with such well-known and enduring singles as 'Sweet Emotion', 'Back In The Saddle', 'Dude (Looks Like A Lady')', 'Ragdoll', 'Cryin'' and 'Pink'. The band are still touring and recording. Tyler even had a stint as an *American Idol* judge.

MARC BOLAN

As the frontman of the iconic glam rock band T-Rex, Marc Bolan is one of Britain's most revered singer-songwriters. He tragically died in a car crash in September 1977. Some of T-Rex's most famous songs include '20th Century Boy', 'Get It On' and 'I Love To Boogie'. Like his friend and rivalry David Bowie, Bolan was also known for his androgynous pretty boy looks.

DAVID BOWIE

A singer-songwriter, actor, record producer and arrange, fashion icon and painter, David Bowie is one of the 20th Century's most enduring cultural icons. Both a household name and an enigma, Bowie has influenced artists in the world of film, fashion, music and art. He has sold 140 million albums, some of his albums include *The Rise And Fall Of Ziggy Stardust And The Spiders From Mars* (1972), *Young Americans* (1975), *Station To Station* (1976) and *Let's Dance* (1983). Bowie declined the royal honour of Commander Of The British Empire in 2000, and also turned down a Knighthood in 2003. Though he is an elusive character, he continues to write, record and release music on a sporadic basis.

MICHAEL JACKSON

The life of Michael Jackson is a tragic one. As one of the most successful and influential pop artists of all time, Jackson's fall from grace was as famous and well-publicised as his rise. He was dubbed the 'King Of Pop' and has influenced many artists from different musical genres, including pop, funk, R&B, rap and rock. His 1982 album *Thriller* is the most successful album of all time while some of his other successful works include *Off The Wall* (1979), *Bad* (1987), *Dangerous* (1991), and *HIStory* (1995). He died on June 25, 2009 aged 50. Regardless of his controversial private life, his music is some of the most popular and respected of all time.

KISS

From New York City, KISS are one of the most successful American rock bands of all time with sales of over 100 million albums. Known for their shock rock image and electrifying stage performances that feature elaborate stage designs and props such as fire breathing, blood spitting, smoking guitars, shooting rockets, glitzy drum kits that levitate, pyro and smoke and all manner of other stage effects, KISS are truly unique. Some of their classic songs include 'Cold Gin', 'Deuce', 'Detroit Rock City', 'Shout It Out Loud' and the ballad 'Beth'. They are one of the most entertaining live bands in the world.

LADY GAGA

Undoubtedly one of the most popular modern day pop stars; a Madonna type artist for her generation. Lady Gaga is a universal icon. She has sold close to 30 million albums worldwide since her 2008 debut, *The Fame*. She has won and been nominated for some of the most coveted prizes in the music biz and been named as one of the world's most influential people by *TIME*. Successful singles include 'Bad Romance', 'Telephone', 'Alejandro', 'Do U Want Me' and 'Applause'.

LED ZEPPELIN

One of the greatest and most revered rock bands of all time, Led Zeppelin remains a huge influence to rock singers the world over. They were not especially popular with critics during their reign but were hugely successful with such albums as *Led Zeppelin* (1969), *Led Zeppelin II* (1969), *Led Zeppelin III* (1970), their untitled fourth album (1971), *Houses of The Holy* (1973), and *Physical Graffiti* (1975). The band consisted of singer Robert Plant, guitarist Jimmy Page, bassist and keyboardist John Paul Jones and the late drummer John Bonham. Their music was a key influence on heavy metal along with the likes of The Who, Cream and The Kinks. Led Zep fused together a variety of genres from folk to blues to rock 'n' roll and psychedlia. They broke up in 1980 after Bonham's premature death. There have been a few one-off reunions since then, notably Live Aid in 1985, 1988 for Atlantic Records' 40th Anniversary Concert and most prominently in 2007 for the Ahmet Ertegun Tribute Concert at the O2 Arena in London with Jason Bonham, John's son, on drums.

MADONNA

As the 'Queen Of Pop' Madonna is a modern cultural icon. Some of her most famous songs include 'Like A Virgin', 'Into The Groove', 'Papa Don't Preach', 'Like A Prayer', 'Vogue', 'Frozen', 'Music', 'Hung Up' and '4 Minutes' and her best-selling albums include *Like A Virgin* (1984), *True Blue* (1986), *Like A Prayer* (1989), *Erotica* (1992) and *Ray Of Light* (1998). She has sold 300 million albums worldwide and founded her own company Maverick. She won a Golden Globe for 'Bets Actress' in the 1996 film *Evita*. She continues to tour and record.

FREDDIE MERCURY

Regularly voted the greatest frontman of all time, Freddie Mercury fronted Queen from 1970 until his death in 1991. Of the 17 songs featured on Queen's *Greatest Hits* album, he wrote ten: 'Bohemian Rhapsody', 'Seven Seas Of Rhye', 'Killer Queen', 'Somebody To Love', 'Good Old-Fashioned Lover Boy', 'We Are The Champions', 'Bicycle Race', 'Don't Stop Me Now', 'Crazy Little Thing Called Love' and 'Play The Game'. He has posthumously been inducted into the Rock And Roll Hall Of Fame, the Songwriters Hall Of Fame, the UK Music Hall Of Fame and the Hollywood Walk Of Fame. A film based on his life is said to be in development. The legend lives on.

QUEEN

Queen are one of the most successful British rock bands of all time with sales of estimated somewhere between 150 and 300 million. They have won just about every major award possible in the music and entertainment industry. They're origins were in glam rock with touches of prog and heavy metal before they became a fully-fledged stadium rock band in the 1980s. They have influenced amongst others, Guns N' Roses, Van Halen, Foo Fighters, The Smashing Pumpkins, Nirvana, Iron Maiden, Anthrax and Dream Theater. Some of their most famous albums include *A Night At The Opera* (1975), *News Of The World* (1977), *The Game* (1980) and *A Kind Of Magic* (1986). The band was comprised of singer Freddie Mercury, guitarist Brian May, drummer Roger Taylor and bassist John Deacon. Between 2004 and 2009 Taylor and May reformed Queen with Bad Company singer Paul Rodgers. They played two world tours and recorded one album, *The Cosmos Rocks*.

RHIANNA

She has sold over 150 million albums worldwide which makes her one of the top selling artists ever. Some of her songs include such universally known tracks as 'Umbrella', 'Take A Bow', 'Disturbia', 'S&M' and 'Stay'. She has won eight Grammy Awards, eight American Music Awards and 22 *Billboard* Music Awards. Like Lady Gaga, she is both a music and fashion icon.

IN HIS OWN WORDS

Here are some press quotes from the man himself.

"I think we need more LGBT artists, that's what I'm hoping we've moved towards, and it looks like things are finally getting to the point where someone who is LGB or T is able to become a recognizable artist, and that's a big step forward, so hopefully we're more and more a part of the entertainment industry."

- **Adam Lambert speaking to *The Backlot* staff, 2014**

"What's happened since then is just surreal to me. It's so crazy that this came out of *American Idol*. I don't think I would have seen it coming back then."

- **Adam Lambert speaking to Andy Greene, *Rolling Stone*, 2014**

"I'm Adam onstage. I'm not playing Freddie. I'm not trying to be him. However, he's so amazing. His recordings and his performances were so incredible that I can't help but be inspired by them."

- **Adam Lambert speaking to Daniel Reynolds, *Advocate*, 2014**

"I've sung other people's music all my life. It's what I did on *American Idol*, and I think one of the things I was known for was making them my own."

- **Adam Lambert speaking to Michael Haan, *The Guardian*, 2012**

"Queen is like one of my all time favourite rock bands, and then to be up on stage with KISS with the pyro and the costumes – I mean, it was a dream come true. It was awesome."

- **Adam Lambert speaking to Adam B. Vary, *Entertainment Weekly*, 2009**

"I feel really creative right now. I feel good. I feel like everything's going to come together and it's going to be a great project."

- **Adam Lambert speaking to Melinda Newman, *Hitfix*, 2011**

"When it first started, I didn't know where to go with it. I didn't know if that minority group even wanted me to be their representative publicly – it seemed almost... presumptuous."

- **Adam Lambert speaking to Caroline Frost, *Huffington Post*, 2012**

"I like a pocket – I like, like, funk or disco or stuff that you can shake your ass to. That's sexy. And this little art car comes zipping by us just blasting Daft Punk."

- **Adam Lambert speaking to Maura Johnston, *Village Voice*, 2012**

"I think, for the majority of my twenties, I was always so concerned with what I didn't have, or what I still wanted."

- **Adam Lambert speaking to *NPR* staff, 2012**

"I'm always listening to what's current – Top 40 for the most part. One of the things we explored on this album was a funkier sensibility."

- **Adam Lambert speaking to Emily Exton, *Popdust*, 2012**

DISCOGRAPHY

This is a selective UK/US discography of Adam Lambert releases…

STUDIO ALBUMS

FOR YOUR ENTERTAINMENT *(CD: RCA, 2009)*

TRESPASSING *(CD: RCA, 2012)*

THE ORIGINAL HIGH *(CD: WARNER BROS, 2015)*

LIVE ALBUMS

GLAM NATION LIVE *(CD: RCA, 2011)*

COMPILATION ALBUMS

TAKE ONE *(CD: RUFFTOWN, 2009)*

THE VERY BEST OF ADAM LAMBERT *(CD: LEGACY, 2014)*

EPs

REMIXES *(DIGITAL: RCA, 2010)*

ACOUSTIC LIVE *(CD: RCA, 2010)*

TRESPASSING EP *(CD: RCA, 2012)*

SINGLES

'NO BOUNDARIES' *(2009)*

'TIME FOR MIRACLES' *(2009)*

'FOR YOUR ENTERTAINMENT' *(2009)*

'WHATAYA WANT FROM ME' *(2009)*

'IF I HAD YOU' *(2010)*

'FEVER' *(2010)*

'SURE FIRE WINNERS' *(2011)*

'AFTERMATH' *(2011)*

'SLEEPWALKER' *(2011)*

'BETTER THAN I KNOW MYSELF' *(2011)*

'NEVER CLOSE OUR EYES' *(2012)*

'TRESPASSING' *(2012)*

OTHER CHARTED SINGLES FEAT. ADAM LAMBERT

'MAD WORLD' *(2009; AMERICAN IDOL SEASON 8)*

'A CHANGE IS GONNA *COME'* *(2009; AMERICAN IDOL SEASON 8)*

'ONE' *(2009; AMERICAN IDOL SEASON 8)*

'CRYIN'' *(2009; AMERICAN IDOL SEASON 8)*

'SLOW RIDE' *(2009; WITH ALLISON IRHTA)*

'THE TRACKS OF MY TEARS' *(2009; AMERICAN IDOL SEASON 8)*

'FEELING GOOD' *(2009; AMERICAN IDOL SEASON 8)*

'CAN'T LET YOU GO' *(2010; FOR YOUR ENTERTAINMENT)*

'MARRY THE NIGHT' *(2013; WITH GLEE CAST)*

COLLABORATIONS

'LIVE THE LIFE' *(2010; J. SCOTT G & ADAM LAMBERT, LIFE THE LIFE EP)*

'LAY ME DOWN' *(2013; AVICII, TRUE)*

MUSIC VIDEOS

'TIME FOR MIRACLES' *(2009; DIR, WAYNE ISHAM)*

'FOR YOUR ENTERTAINMENT' *(2009; DIR, RAY KAY)*

'WHATAYA WANT FROM ME' *(2009; DIR, DIANE MARTEL)*

'IF I HAD YOU' *(2010; DIR, BRYAN BARBER)*

'BETTER THAN I KNOW MYSELF' *(2011; DIR, RAY KAY)*

'NEVER CLOSE OUR EYES' *(2012; DIR, DORI OSKOWITZ)*

TOURS

AMERICAN IDOLS LIVE! TOUR *(2009)*

GLAM NATION TOUR *(2010)*

QUEEN + ADAM LAMBERT TOUR *(2012)*

WE ARE GLAMILY TOUR *(2013)*

QUEEN + ADAM LAMBERT TOUR *(2014-2015)*

APPENDECIES

BIBLIOGRAPHY & SOURCES

The following books, magazines and websites were integral in the making of this book. I remain deeply indebted to them all.

MAGAZINES

Classic Rock

Fireworks

Metal Hammer

Powerplay

Record Collector

NEWSPAPERS

Daily Mirror

Daily Telegraph

Guardian

Independent

LA Times

New York Times

Observer

WEBSITES

www.advocate.com

www.allmusic.com

www.thebacklot.com

wwww.billboard.com

http://blogcritics.org

www.bostonmagazine.com

www.brumlive.com

www.classicrockrevisited.com

www.cosmik.com

www.craveonline.com

http://dailyreview.crikey.com.au

www.dallasvoice.com

www.details.com

www.digitalspy.co.uk

www.emusic.com

www.entertainmentweekly.com

www.ew.com

www.express.co.uk

http://gc.guitarcenter.com

www.glidemagazine.com

www.goldminemag.com

www.grammy.com

www.guitarworld.com

www.hollywoodreporter.com

www.hitfix.com

www.holymoley.com

www.thehothits.com

www.huffingtonpost.co.uk

www.idolator.com

http://indulge-sound.com

http://liverockjournal.com

www.jewishjournal.com

http://kingsofar.com

http://laslush.com

interview/www.manchestereveningnews.co.uk

www.menshealth.com

www.metal-rules.com

www.metal-temple.com

www.miami.com

www.mirror.co.uk

www.mtv.com

www.musicradar.com

www.newsday.com

www.noise101.com

www.npr.org

www.nydailynews.com

www.out.com

http://popdust.com

www.popmatters.com

www.premierguitar.com

http://radio.com

www.rockcellarmagazine.com

www.rockmusicstar.com

www.rockoveramerica.com

http://rockrevoltmagazine.com

www.rollingstone.com

www.ryanseacrest.com

http://seattletimes.com

www.slantmagazine.com

www.sleazeroxx.com

www.songfacts.com

http://southfloridagaynews.com

www.technologytell.com

www.todayonline.com

http://ultimateclassicrock.com

http://usatoday.com

www.vanyaland.com

www.vh1.com

http://blogs.villagevoice.com

www.vintageguitar.com

www.washingtonpost.com

www.womansday.com

ADAM LAMBERT WEBSITES

www.adamlambert.com

http://theadamlambertconnection.com

ACKNOWLEDGEMENTS

Thank you to the following writers whose work I have quoted in this book. I am deeply indebted to them all. Their articles, reviews and interviews have provided invaluable insight into Adam Lambert's life and music:

Thank you to the following folks for their input: *Steve Baltin, Erika Berlin, Misha Berson, Matthew Breen, Fred Bronson, Jim Cantiello, Jon Caramanica, Paul Cashmere, Tim Chipping, Howard Cohen, Michelle Collins, Robert Copsey, Kevin Coughlin, Robbie Daw, Farah Daley, Angela Ebron, Stephen Thomas Erlewine, Emily Exton, Jim Farber, Katie Fitzpatrick, Caroline Frost, Glenn Gamboa, Catherine Gee, Irina Gordon, Leah Greenblatt, Andy Greene, Vanessa Grigoriadis, Shirley Halperin, Michael Haan, Nicky Horne, Paul Jeeves, Maura Johnston, Arnold Wayne Jones, Jonathan Keefe, Pam Kragen, Shana Naomi Krochmal, Lina Lecaro, Jason Lipshutz, Brian Mansfield, Dan Martin, Sierra Marquina, Ruth McCann, Neil McCormick, Ben Neutze Melinda Newman, Gelb Olkhovo, Naomi Pfefferman,*

James Poniewozik, Ann Powers, Sophia Rahman, Amelia Raitt, Guy Raz, Daniel Reynolds, Nancy Jo Sales, Rob Sheffield, Dave Simpson, Tanner Stransky, Caroline Sullivan, Eddie Trunk, Adam B. Vary, Matt Wardlaw, Emma Webb, Annie Zaleski and *Gail Zimmerman.*

The following websites proved invaluable: *All Music, Billboard, Boston Magazine, Brum Live, Classic Rock Revisited, Cosmik Debris, Crave Online, Digital Spy, Entertainment Weekly, Glide Magazine, Goldmine, Grammy.com, Guitar Center, Guitar World, Holy Moley, Hollywood Reporter, Kings Of A&R, LA Slush, Live Rock Journal, Men's Health, Metal Rules, Metal Temple, Miami.com, MTV.com, Music Radar, Newsday, Noise 101, Pop Matters, Premier Guitar, Radio.com, Rock Cellar Magazine, Rock Music Star, Rock Over America, Rock Revolt Magazine, Rolling Stone, Slant Magazine, Sleaze Roxx, Song Facts, South Florida Gay News, Technology Tell, Today Online, TV Guide, Ultimate Classic Rock, USA Today, Vanyaland, Vintage Guitar* and *Womans Day.*

The following printed music magazines proved invaluable:

Classic Rock, Fireworks, Metal Hammer, Powerplay and *Record Collector.*

The following printed newspapers proved invaluable: *Daily Express, Daily Mirror, Daily Telegraph, The Guardian, Independent, LA Times, Manchester Evening News, New York Daily News, New York Times, North County Times, The Observer, People, Seattle Time, TIME, Toronto Post* and *Washington Post.*

Apologies if I have missed out any names. It was not intentional!

DISCLAIMER

The author gratefully acknowledges permission to quote and use references from the sources as referenced in the main text and repeated in the *Bibliography*. Every quote and reference taken from selected sources is fully acknowledged in the main text and in the *Bibliography & Sources* and *Acknowledgements*.

However, it has not been entirely possible to contact every copyright holder, but every effort has been made to contact all copyright holders and to clear reprint permissions from the list of sources. If notified, the publishers/author will be pleased to rectify any omission in future editions. The opinions of the contributing writers/journalists do not reflect those of the author.

ABOUT THE AUTHOR

NEIL DANIELS has written about rock and metal for a wide range of magazines, fanzines and websites. He has written over a dozen books on such artists as Judas Priest, Rob Halford, Bon Jovi, Linkin Park, Journey, Bryan Adams, Joe Perry, Neal Schon, Richie Sambora, Brian May, Iron Maiden, You Me At Six, Metallica, AC/DC, Pantera, UFO, ZZ Top and Robert Plant. He also co-authored *Dawn Of The Metal Gods: My Life In Judas Priest And Heavy Metal* with original Judas Priest singer/co-founder Al Atkins. His third book on Judas Priest is the CD sized *Rock Landmarks – Judas Priest's British Steel*, published by Wymer.

His acclaimed series, *All Pens Blazing – A Rock And Heavy Metal Writer's Handbook Volumes I & II,* collects over a hundred original and exclusive interviews with some of the world's most famous rock and metal scribes.

His second duel collection of rock writings, *Rock 'N' Roll Mercenaries – Interviews With Rock Stars Volumes I & II,* compiles sixty interviews with many well-known rock stars and scribes. The former collections were republished via Createspace as *Rock 'N' Roll Sinners* while the latter books were republished in an omnibus edition titled, *Hard Rock Rebels – Talking With Rock Stars*.

His Createspace books are *AOR Chronicles, Rock & Metal Chronicles, Hard Rock Rebels – Talking With Rock Stars, Rock 'N' Roll Sinners – Volumes I, II & III, Rock Bites, Love It Loud, Get Your Rock On – Melodic Rock Shots, Bang Your Head – Heavy Metal Shots, In A Dark Room – Exploits Of A Genre Fan* and the fictional rock 'n' roll novel, *It's My Life*.

His books have so far been translated into Brazilian, Bulgarian, Czech, Finnish, French, German, Italian, Japanese, Polish and Swedish with more foreign titles in the works.

His reviews, articles and interviews on rock music and pop culture have been published in *The Guardian, Classic Rock Presents AOR, Classic Rock Presents Let It Rock, Rock Sound, Record Collector, Big Cheese, Powerplay, Fireworks, MediaMagazine, Rocktopia.co.uk, Get Ready To Rock.com, Lucemfero.com, musicOMH.com, Ghostcultmag.com, Drowned In Sound.com, BBCNewsOnline.co.uk, Carling.com, Unbarred.co.uk* and *Planet Sound* on Channel4's Teletext service. He has also written several sets of sleeve notes for Angel Air and BGO Records.

His website is ***www.neildanielsbooks.com***

PUBLISHED BOOKS BY NEIL DANIELS

MUSIC BIOGRAPHIES

The Story Of Judas Priest – Defenders Of The Faith

(Omnibus Press, 2007).

Robert Plant – Led Zeppelin, Jimmy Page And The Solo Years

(Independent Music Press, 2008).

Bon Jovi Encyclopaedia

(Chrome Dreams, 2009).

Dawn Of The Metal Gods – My Life In Judas Priest And Heavy Metal **(with Al Atkins)**

(Iron Pages, 2009).

Linkin Park – An Operator's Manual

(Chrome Dreams, 2009).

Don't Stop Believin' – The Untold Story Of Journey

(Omnibus Press, 2011).

Rock Landmarks – Judas Priest's British Steel

(Wymer Publishing, 2011).

Metallica – The Early Years And The Rise Of Metal

(Independent Music Press, 2012).

Iron Maiden – The Ultimate Unauthorised History Of The Beast

(Voyageur Press, 2012).

You Me At Six – Never Hold An Underdog Down

(Independent Music Press, 2012).

AC/DC – The Early Years With Bon Scott

(Independent Music Press, 2013).

Reinventing Metal – The True Story Of Pantera And The
Tragically Short Life Of Dimebag Darrell

(Backbeat Books, 2013).

High Stakes & Dangerous Men – The UFO Story

(Soundcheck Books, 2013).

Beer Drinkers & Hell Raisers – A ZZ Top Guide

(Soundcheck Books, 2014).

Killers – The Origins Of Iron Maiden: 1975-1983

(Soundcheck Books, 2014).

Let It Rock – The Making Of Bon Jovi's Slippery When Wet

(Soundcheck Books, 2014).

FILM BIOGRAPHIES

Matthew McConaughey – The Biography

(John Blake, 2014).

The Unexpected Adventures Of Martin Freeman

(John Blake, 2015).

CASUAL GUIDES

Electric World – A Casual Guide To The Music Of Journey's Neal Schon

(Createspace, 2014).

Reckless – A Casual Guide To The Music Of Bryan Adams

(Createspace, 2014).

Stranger In This Town – A Casual Guide To The Music Of Bon Jovi's Richie Sambora

(Createspace, 2014).

Made Of Metal – A Casual Guide To The Solo Music Of Judas Priest's Rob Halford

(Createspace, 2014).

Back To The Light – A Casual Guide To The Music Of Queen's Brian May

(Createspace, 2015).

Once A Rocker, Always A Rocker – A Casual Guide To The

Music Of Aerosmith's Joe Perry

(Createspace, 2015).

COLLECTED WORKS

All Pens Blazing – A Rock And Heavy Metal Writer's Handbook

Volume I

(AuthorsOnline, 2009).

All Pens Blazing – A Rock And Heavy Metal Writer's Handbook

Volume II

(AuthorsOnline, 2010).

Rock 'N' Roll Mercenaries – Interviews With Rock Stars Volume

I

(AuthorsOnline, 2010).

Rock 'N' Roll Mercenaries – Interviews With Rock Stars Volume

II

(AuthorsOnline, 2011).

CREATESPACE

AOR Chronicles – Volume 1

(Createspace, 2013).

Rock & Metal Chronicles – Volume 1

(Createspace, 2013).

Hard Rock Rebels – Talking With Rock Stars

(Createspace, 2013).

Rock 'N' Roll Sinners – Volume I

(Createspace, 2013).

Rock 'N' Roll Sinners – Volume II

(Createspace, 2013).

Rock 'N' Roll Sinners – Volume III

(Createspace, 2013).

Rock Bites

(Createspace, 2013).

Love It Loud

(Createspace, 2013).

Get Your Rock On – Melodic Rock Shots

(Createspace, 2013).

Bang Your Head – Heavy Metal Shots

(Createspace, 2013).

In A Dark Room – Exploits Of A Genre Fan

(Createspace, 2013).

FICTION

It's My Life – A (Fictional) Rock 'N' Roll Memoir

(Createspace, 2013).

PRAISE FOR THE AUTHOR'S PREVIOUS WORKS

"Neil Daniels is great on the early years of Brummie metal legends Judas Priest..."

- *Classic Rock* on **The Story Of Judas Priest – Defenders Of The Faith**

"'I've never reached the top...but I gave it a bloody good go!' says original Judas Priest singer Al Atkins in the introduction to his autobiography. With a foreword by Judas Priest bassist Ian Hill ... Metal Gods *covers the pre-fame years of the second-ever metal band in entertaining detail."*

- *Metal Hammer* on **Dawn Of The Metal Gods – My Life In Judas Priest And Heavy Metal**

"The book also has a curious appendices exploring – among other things – Percy's interest in folklore and mythology."

- *Mojo* on **Robert Plant – Led Zeppelin, Jimmy Page And The Solo Years**

"Prolific rock and metal author Neil Daniels does a very good job

in detailing a veritable smorgasbord of the events, places, people, releases and merchandises of the band, the writer displaying his customary attention to detail and enthusiasm for accuracy."

- *Record Collector* on **Bon Jovi Encyclopaedia**

"...in terms of writing, content and presentation I think it's probably his best... Linkin Park - An Operator's Manual *is an attractive book with black and white photos on every page."*

- *Fireworks* on **Linkin Park – An Operator's Manual**

"... the aggregate of this book is an at minimum interesting and at max fascinating read for any rock fan, 'cos you get the whole deal, the history of Sounds, Kerrang!, Metal Hammer, BW&BK, *all the mags, plus the mechanics of book writing, and more mainstream, who's a good interview and bad plus proof, crazy road stories...friggin' well all of this would be interesting to any rocker. Period."*

- *Bravewords.com* on **All Pens Blazing – A Rock And Heavy Metal Writer's Handbook Volume I**

"But once again, this rollercoaster ride through some of rock's back pages will bring a glow to the cheek, and perhaps even moistness to the mouth, of any self-respecting rock fan who has ever bought a music paper or mag since the 1970s."

- *Get Ready To Rock*.com on **All Pens Blazing – A Rock And Heavy Metal Writer's Handbook Volume II**

"These two volumes of interviews celebrate the art of rock journalism."

- *Classic Rock* on **All Pens Blazing – A Rock And Heavy Metal Writer's Handbook Volumes 1 & 11**

"As a lone-time yet casual fan of the band, I found the band's story very interesting and quite surprising... I received the book on Thursday, used every possible opportunity to read it and finished it on Sunday. That's a recommendation if any."

- *Rock United*.com on **Don't Stop Believin' – The Untold Story Of Journey**

"With a track by track analysis, tour dates and photos from the

period this is everything you needed to know about what is arguably Priest's finest thirty-odd minutes wrapped up into in one handy bite sized paperback at a budget price."

- *Sea Of Tranquility.org* on **Rock Landmarks – Judas Priest's British Steel**

"It's an insightful look at one of metal's most important bands, and though there have been many books written about them, Metallica have never seemed as easy to understand as after reading this."

- *Curled Up.com* on **Metallica – The Early Years And The Rise Of Metal**

"In all, Daniels has crafted a very high-level and easy read with Iron Maiden - The Ultimate Unauthorized History Of The Beast, *and top it all off, it's packaged expertly, prime for your coffee table, where Eddie's piercing eyes await."*

- *Blistering.com* on **Iron Maiden – The Ultimate Unauthorised History Of The Beast**

"This book was a great read. 154 pages crammed with the wonderfully written story of You Me At Six... With some lovely photos and a very handy discography at the back, You Me At Six – Never Hold An Underdog Down *is a must have for any YMAS fan."*

- *Get Ready To Rock.com* on **You Me At Six – Never Hold An Underdog Down**

"Daniels style is engaging and covers in excellent detail the first six years of the band...Each chapter covers a year and Daniels provides great detail on the various Australian vs. International pressings of the first few albums. It's very detailed and well researched."

- *Metal-Rules.com* on **AC/DC – The Early Years With Bon Scott**

"The tours, the music, the fun, the life, and the death, of one of the best metal acts of the '90s...it's all here. Nice job once again by Mr. Daniels."

- *Sea Of Tranquility.org* on **Reinventing Metal – The True Story Of Pantera And The Tragically Short Life Of**

Dimebag Darrell

"Overall, I wouldn't hesitate to recommend this book to not only the diehards (who will snap it up anyway), but also those who want to delve just a little further than Michael Schenker, Phil Mogg (who emerges as quite the dictatorial figure in places), and the band's often horrendous choice of stage outfits!"

- *Classic Rock Society* on **High Stakes & Dangerous Men – The UFO Story**

"The book is an insight into the group's rise to fame, the funny times and their rise to become iconic bearded rocking heroes. I really enjoyed the section on ZZ Top trivia, there's funny and intriguing examples to make you smile and laugh out loud."

- *The Mayfair Mall Zine.com* on **Beer Drinkers & Hell Raisers – A ZZ Top Guide**

"This is a book for the superfan, to be honest. But for the superfan, it is a fantastic volume collecting a ton of information on a great player that you wouldn't be able to find in one place otherwise."

- *Music Tomes.com* on **Electric World – A Casual Guide To The Music Of Journey's Neal Schon**

"...if you thought you knew everything there was to know about Iron Maiden, then think again, as Daniels manages to turn up nugget after nugget of trivia and fact. This is a very rewarding read and I would wholeheartedly recommend this to any rock music fan, in fact buy it now and pack it away in your suitcase for your summer holiday read."

- *Planet Mosh.com* on **Killers – The Origins Of Iron Maiden: 1975-1983**

"Told in straightforward language and amazingly concise as for the time span it covers, Let It Rock: The Making Of Bon Jovi's Slippery When Wet *is a fine, solid work."*

- *Hardrock Heaven* on **Let It Rock – The Making Of Bon Jovi's Slippery When Wet**

"...Mr Daniels has applied his knack of bringing you right into the subject here and Bryan Adams fans will love Reckless - A Casual Guide To The Music Of Bryan Adams.*"*

- *Get Ready To Rock* on **Reckless – A Casual Guide To The Music Of Bryan Adams**

"Made Of Metal *is a excellent guide to the long, sometimes magnificent, sometimes frustrating, sometimes downright horrible solo career of the Metal God.*"

- *Metal-Rules* on **Made Of Metal – A Casual Guide To The Solo Music Of Judas Priest's Rob Halford**

Visit

www.neildanielsbooks.com

ALSO AVAILABLE FROM

NEIL DANIELS BOOKS

PUBLISHED BY

CREATESPACE

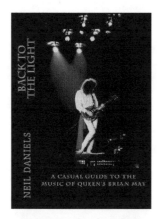

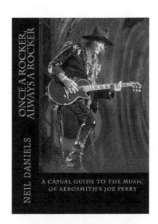

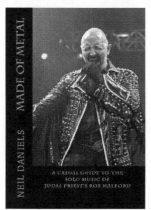

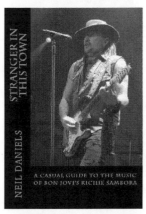

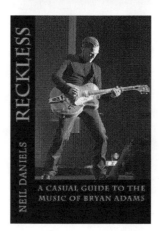

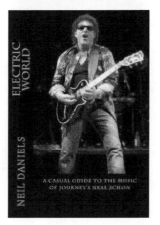

AOR CHRONICLES - VOLUME 1
NEIL DANIELS

Rock & Metal Chronicles - Volume 1
Neil Daniels

HARD ROCK REBELS - TALKING WITH ROCK STARS
Neil Daniels

Bang Your Head - Heavy Metal Shots
Neil Daniels

Get Your Rock On - Melodic Rock Shots
Neil Daniels

LOVE IT LOUD
Neil Daniels

ROCK 'N' ROLL SINNERS - VOLUME I
Neil Daniels

ROCK 'N' ROLL SINNERS - VOLUME II
Neil Daniels

ROCK 'N' ROLL SINNERS - VOLUME III
Neil Daniels

KILLER QUEEN

Photos by Chris Mee, 2015

Photos by Chris Mee, 2015

Photos by Chris Mee, 2015

Photos by Chris Mee, 2015

Photos by Chris Mee, 2015

Photos by Chris Mee, 2015

Photos by Chris Mee, 2015

Photos by Chris Mee, 2015

Photos by Chris Mee, 2015

NEIL DANIELS BOOKS

AUTHOR / CRITIC / MUSIC JOURNALIST / WRITER

QUALITY BOOKS ON ROCK & METAL MUSIC AND

POP CULTURE

For details on Neil Daniels Books visit:

www.neildanielsbooks.com

Manufactured by Amazon.ca
Bolton, ON

33212855R00155